Painting of Stage Setting for the New York Production by Jo Mielziner. Copyright, 1954, by Jo Mielziner. The publisher gratefully acknowledges Mr. Mielziner's permission to reproduce this drawing in the present living

CAT ON A HOT TIN ROOF

A PLAY IN THREE ACTS
BY TENNESSEE WILLIAMS

★

DRAMATISTS
PLAY SERVICE
INC.

CAT ON A HOT TIN ROOF was presented at the Morosco Theatre in New York City on March 24, 1955, by The Playwrights' Company. It was directed by Elia Kazan; the stage set was designed by Jo Mielziner, and the cast was as follows:

LACEY .... Maxwell Glanville

SOOKEY .... Musa Williams

MARGARET .... Barbara Bel Geddes

BRICK .... Ben Gazzara

MAE, *sometimes called "Sister Woman"* .... Madeline Sherwood

GOOPER, *sometimes called "Brother Man"* .... Pat Hingle

BIG MAMA .... Mildred Dunnock

DIXIE .... Pauline Hahn

BUSTER .... Darryl Richard

SONNY .... Seth Edwards

TRIXIE .... Janice Dunn

BIG DADDY .... Burl Ives

REVEREND TOOKER .... Fred Stewart

DOCTOR BAUGH .... R. G. Armstrong

DAISY .... Eva Vaughan Smith

BRIGHTIE .... Brownie McGhee

SMALL .... Sonny Terry

SCENE: A bed-sitting room and section of the gallery of a plantation home in the Mississippi Delta, an evening in summer. The action is continuous, with two intermissions.

Cat on a Hot Tin Roof

ACT I

When the house lights go out, a group of voices, young-sters and adults, can be heard singing a merry, old-fash-ioned Southern song. The lights on stage commence to build, and the traveler opens. The scene is a bed-sitting room and section of the gallery of a plantation home in the Mississippi Delta. It is early evening in summer.
TIME: *The present.*
The room is raked at a forward pitch and one corner of the room just past the proscenium and into the orchestra. The central playing area is roughly diamond-shaped, and it is surrounded upstage and downstage at the R. by a duckboard gallery walk, slightly lower than the level of the room. Across the back of this gallery, five columns, indicated by velour-covered strips (shadowing the im-aginary flutes in the columns), through which the dark-ening evening sky is seen. Up L., a platform level with the room, leads off into the hall. Down L., a shuttered bathroom door stands open. Doors to the room are im-aginary. They are up L. C., into the hall: down R., onto the gallery, and down stage R., to the lower part of the gallery. A double-bed with a curious wicker headpiece representing giant cornucopiae, is in the up R. corner of the room. A wicker night table is at the L. of the bed. In the upper L. corner of the room is a huge, modern style bar unit with built-in radio and TV. This is known as "Echo Spring," taking its name from the bottles of Southern bourbon that adorn it. Down R., a plain, flat couch supports a single, white pillow at its head, a neatly-folded gray blanket at its foot. There is but one pillow on the bed. Between the foot of the bed and the couch,

a wicker love-seat faces c. stage, and a bit front. The floor of the room is covered with a flowered carpet. On the ceiling is a rococo painting representing two cupids in flight.

During the singing, Lacey, a Negro handyman, appears in the lawn area, upstage, between the upper gallery and the sky-drop. He ambles from R. toward L., carrying two dust-covered wine bottles, and humming the tune of the song to himself. His progress is interrupted by the urgent voice of Sookey, a Negro maid.

SOOKEY. (*Off* U. L.) Lacey! Lacey!

LACEY. Yeah—I'm comin'.

SOOKEY. (*Hurrying in from* U. L. *to meet Lacey.*) Oh—Lacey!

LACEY. All right—I'm comin'.

SOOKEY. Come on, boy—they waitin' for this stuff! (*Sookey takes the wine bottles from Lacey and hurries off* L. *He follows slowly. Off* L., *a disturbance is heard in the singing. A young woman's voice complains loudly that someone has thrown a hot buttered-biscuit on her dress, and that the dress is ruined. The singing resumes. Margaret enters from the hall* L. *in a pretty white dress. She pauses in front of the bar, examining a spot on the front of the skirt. She steps downstage to the* R. *side of the room's point, and looks into an imaginary mirror. The light in the room is too dim for her to see the dress clearly. She moves to the* U. R. *imaginary gallery doors, and pantomimes opening the doors. Light builds in the playing area. Margaret returns to the mirror. As she studies her dress, she calls over her* L. *shoulder toward the bathroom.*)

MARGARET. Brick! Brick—one of those no-neck monsters hits me with a hot buttered biscuit, so I have t' change!

BRICK. (*Calls from bathroom, off* L.) Wha'd you say, Maggie? Water was on s' loud I couldn't hear ya. . . .

MARGARET. Well, I—just remarked that—one of th' no-neck monsters messed up m' lovely lace dress, so I got t' change. . . . (*She crosses* U. C. *and gets out of the dress, puts it on wicker seat. Brick reaches out of the bathroom toward the bar for a drink. He is wrapped in a tan bathrobe, and his* R. *foot is in a plaster cast, with a steel foot-rest built-in.*)

BRICK. Why d'ya call Gooper's kiddies no-neck monsters?

MARGARET. Because they've got no necks! Isn't that a good enough reason?

BRICK. (*Drinking.*) Don't they have any necks?

MARGARET. None visible. (*Brick retires to the bathroom with his drink.*) Their fat little heads are set on their fat little bodies without a bit of connection. (*Sonny followed by Buster followed by Dixie enter lawn* U. L., *running across to* C., *fighting. Mae enters* L., *calls them back off* L. *Gooper calls them off from off* L.) Hear them? Hear them screaming? (*Cross to* R. *of bed.*) I don't know where their voice boxes are located, since they've got no necks. I tell you, I got so nervous at that table tonight, I thought I'd throw back my head and utter a howl you could hear across the Arkansas border. (*Margaret flops across the bed on her back, her head toward* C. *She toys with a palmetto fan that has been lying on the bed.*) I said to your charming sister-in-law, Mae— honey, couldn't you feed those precious little things at a separate table with an oilcloth cover? They make such a mess an' the lace cloth looks so pretty. (*She sits up.*) She made enormous eyes at me and said, "Ohhh, noooo! On Big Daddy's birthday? Why, he would never forgive me!" (*Flops onto her stomach.*) Well, I want you to know, Big Daddy hasn't been at the table two minutes with those five no-neck monsters slobbering and drooling over their food before he threw down his fork an' shouted, "Fo' God's sake, Gooper, why don't you put them pigs at a trough in the kitchen?" Well, I swear, I simply could have di-ieed! (*Brick enters* D. L., *hobbling with a crutch under his* R. *arm. He has a towel wrapped around his neck. On his* L. *foot, a bedroom slipper. He goes to the bar to replenish his drink. Margaret, on her belly, looking at Brick.*) Think of it, Brick, they've got five of them and number six is coming. They've brought the whole bunch down here like animals to display at the county fair. Why, they have those children doin' tricks all the time! "Junior, show Big Daddy how you do this—show Big Daddy how you do that; say your piece fo' Big Daddy, Sister. Brother, show Big Daddy how you stand on your head! Show your dimples, Sugar!"—It goes on all the time, along with constant little remarks and innuendoes about the fact that you and I have not produced any children, are totally child- less and therefore totally useless! (*They exchange a brief look. He continues fixing his drink.*) Of course it's comical, but it's also disgusting, since it's so obvious what they're up to! (*Off* U. L.,

7

*Big Daddy reaches the tag-line of one of his famous stories:
"Jesus! Looks like a coupla elephants in heat!" This is greeted
with general laughter and ad lib.)*
BRICK. What are they up to, Maggie?
MARGARET. Why, you know what they're up to! *(Brick lounges
against the bar, drying his hair with the towel. Margaret, sitting
up.)* I'll tell you what they're up to, boy of mine!—they're up to
cutting you out of your father's estate, and now that we know Big
Daddy's—dyin' of—cancer. *(Off* U. L., *on the words "Big Daddy"
in Margaret's speech, Big Daddy makes another humorous sally,
which is gretted with considerable response.)*
BRICK. *(Looking at Margaret.)* Do we? Do we know Big Daddy's
dyin' of cancer?
MARGARET. Got the report today.
BRICK. Oh.
MARGARET. Yep, got the report just now. It didn't surprise me,
Baby. I recognized the symptoms soon's we got here last spring,
and I'm willin' to bet you that Brother Man and his wife were
pretty sure of it, too. That more than likely explains why their
usual summer migration to the coolness of the Great Smokies was
passed up this summer in favor of hustlin' down here ev'ry whip-
stitch with their whole screamin' tribe! And that's why so many
allusions have been made to Silver Hill lately. *(Rises by the foot
of the bed.)* You know what Silver Hill is? Place that's famous
for treatin' alcoholics an' dope-fiends in the movies!
BRICK. *(Hobbling through* C. *to* D. R.*)* I'm not in the movies.
MARGARET. *(Crosses* C.*)* No, and you don't take dope. Otherwise, you're a perfect candidate for Silver Hill, Baby, and that's
where they aim to ship you. *(Brick moves to the step leading onto
the lower gallery,* D. R., *and stands, looking out. Margaret crosses
to his shoulder.)* Then Brother Man could get a-hold of the purse
strings and dole out remittances to us, maybe get power-of-at-
torney and sign checks for us and cut off our credit wherever,
whenever he wanted! How'd you like that, Baby? *(A step* C., *she
turns to Brick.)* Well, you've been doin' just about everything in
your power to bring it about, you've just been doin' ev'rything
you can think of to aid and abet them in this scheme of theirs:
Quittin' work, devotin' yourself to the occupation of drinkin'!
Breakin' your ankle last night on the high school athletic field:
doin' what? Jumpin' hurdles! At two or three in the mornin'! Just

8

fantastic! Got in the paper. Clarksdale *Register* carried a nice little item about it, human interest story about a well-known former athlete stagin' a one-man track-meet on the high school athletic field last night—(*Moves toward Brick, a bit above him.*) but was slightly out of condition and didn't clear the first hurdle! Brother Man Gooper claims he exercised his influence t' keep it from goin' out over AP and UP an' every other dam' P! (*She crosses to his shoulder.*) But, Brick—(*Brick steps onto the gallery, and moves away a bit, D. L.*) you still have one big advantage ——

BRICK. Did you say something, Maggie?

MARGARET. (*Behind him.*) Big Daddy dotes on you, honey. And he can't stand Brother Man and Brother Man's wife, that monster of fertility, Mae—she's downright odious to him! Know how I know? By little expressions that flicker over his face when that woman is holdin' fo'th on one of her choice topics—(*Crosses D. C. toward audience.*) such as—how she refused twilight sleep when the twins were delivered! Because she feels motherhood's an experience that a woman ought to experience fully!—in order to fully appreciate the "wonder and beauty of it!" HAH! (*Crosses D. L. a step.*) an' how she made Brother Man come in an' stand beside her in the delivery room so he would not miss out on the "wonder and beauty of it" either!—producin' those no-neck monsters! (*She crosses to bar, gets an ice-cube from the ice bucket, and commences to rub her arms with the ice. She turns, facing front.*) Big Daddy shares my attitude toward those two! As for me, well—I give him a laugh now and then and he tolerates me. In fact—I sometimes suspect that Big Daddy harbors a little unconscious "lech" for me.

BRICK. What makes you think Big Daddy has a lech for you, Maggie?

MAGGIE. (*Sliding the ice-cube between her breasts as she speaks.*) Why, he always drops his eyes down my body when I'm talkin' to him, drops his eyes to my boobs an' licks his old chops! BRICK. That kind of talk is disgusting.

MARGARET. (*Drops ice-cube on bar, leans against bar, facing front.*) Did anyone ever tell you that you're an ass-aching Puritan, Brick? I think it's mighty fine that that ole fellow, on the doorstep of death, still takes in my shape with what I think is deserved appreciation! (*Off U. L., there are more screams and howls from the children, and again adults attempt to quell the battle. Brick crosses*

9

to bar and puts ice in his glass and pours more bourbon for himself. Margaret crosses to bed. Brick faces front, drinking. Margaret picks up pillow from bed, sits on L. *side of bed, facing Brick, and holding the pillow in her arms.*) Yes, sir, Baby, you should of been at that supper-table. Y'know, Big Daddy, bless his ole sweet soul, he's the dearest ole thing in the world, but he does hunch over his food as if he preferred not to notice anything else. Well, Mae an' Gooper were side by side at the table, direckly across from Big Daddy, watchin' his face like hawks while they jawed an' jabbered about the cuteness an' brilliance of the no-neck monsters! And the no-neck monsters were ranged around the table, some in high-chairs and some on th' Books of Knowledge, all in fancy little paper caps in honor of Big Daddy's birthday, and all through dinner, well, I want you to know that Brother Man an' his wife never once, for one moment, stopped exchanging pokes an' pinches an' kicks an' signs an' signals! (*Brick rests his crutch against the bar. He rolls up his towel and rubs it through his hair and against his forehead.*) Even Big Mama, bless her ole sweet soul, she isn't th' quickest an' brightest thing in the world, she finally noticed at last, an' said, "Gooper, what are you an' Mae makin' all these signs at each other about?" I swear t' God, I nearly choked on my chicken! (*Brick gives Margaret a look. Softly, arrested by his expression.*) What?

BRICK. (*With an easy gesture.*) Nothing. (*Margaret puts the pillow on the bed. She rumples her hair, rises, goes to the night stand for a comb. Brick continues to rub himself with the towel. He is still standing by the bar.*)

MARGARET. Y' know, your brother Gooper still cherishes the illusion he took a giant step up on the social ladder when he married Miss Mae Flynn of the Memphis Flynns. (*Crosses* D. R. C., *looks in mirror, combing hair.*) But I have a piece of Spanish news for Gooper. The Flynns never had a thing in this world but money, and they lost that. They were nothin' at all but fairly successful climbers. Of course Mae Flynn came out in Memphis eight years before I made my debut in Nashville, but I had friends at Ward-Belmont who came from Memphis, and they used to come to see me and I used to go to see them for Christmas an' spring vacations, so I know who rates an' who doesn't rate in Memphis society. (*Brick puts the towel on the bar and picks up his drink. From time to time, he sips from the glass, slowly, easily. Margaret, looking*

10

into the mirror.) Why, y'know, ole Papa Flynn, he barely escaped doin' time in the Federal pen for shady manipulations on th' stock market when his chain-stores crashed, and as for Mae havin' been a cotton carnival queen, as they remind us so often, lest we forget, well, that's one honor I don't envy her for! Sit on a brass throne, on a tacky float an' ride down Main Street, smilin', bowin' an' blowin' kisses to all the trash on the street! Why, year before last, when Susan McPheeters was singled out fo' that honor, y'know what happened to her? Y'know what happened to poor little Susie McPheeters?

BRICK. No. What happened to little Susie McPheeters?

MARGARET. Somebody spit tobacco juice in her face.

BRICK. Somebody spit tobacco juice in her face? (*He drinks.*)

MARGARET. That's right, some ole drunk leaned out of a window in the Hotel Gayoso an' yelled, "Hey! hey! hey there, Queenie!" Poor Susie looked up an' flashed him a radiant smile— (*Smiles at Brick over her shoulder.*) an' he shot a squirt of tobacco juice right in poor Susie's face! (*Again she looks into the mirror.*)

BRICK. (*Crosses to above L. of Margaret, carrying drink.*) Well, what d'you know about that?

MARGARET. (*Gaily.*) What do I know about it? I was there! I saw it!

BRICK. (*Leans on his crutch, studying Margaret.*) Must have been kind of funny.

MARGARET. Susie didn't think so. Had hysterics. Screamed like a banshee. They had to stop the parade an' remove her —— (*She catches sight of Brick in the mirror, and gasps slightly. He starts to whistle "By the Light of the Silvery Moon." She wheels to face Brick.*) Why are you looking at me like that?

BRICK. Like what, Maggie? (*Resumes whistling.*)

MARGARET. The way y' were lookin' at me just now befo' I caught your eye in the mirror and you started t' whistle! I don't know how to describe it, but it froze my blood! (*Turns away R., then U. S.*) I've caught you lookin' at me like that so often lately. What are you thinkin' of when you look at me like that? (*She crosses to below bar.*)

BRICK. (*Holds.*) I wasn't conscious of lookin' at you, Maggie.

MARGARET. Well, I was conscious of it! What were you thinkin'?

BRICK. I don't remember thinkin' of anything, Maggie.

11

MARGARET. (*Crosses above Brick to* C.) Don't you think I know that ——? Don't you think I—know that ——?

BRICK. Know *what*, Maggie?

MARGARET. (*Crosses* D. L., *facing audience from* D. L. *side of room.*) That I've gone through this—*hideous*—*transformation*—become—*hard! Frantic! Cruel!* (*Looks at Brick.*) That's what you've been observing in me lately. How could y' help but observe it? That's all right. I'm not thin-skinned any more, can't afford to be thin-skinned any more. But, Brick—Brick —— (*Brick hobbles* R. *in the room, below the wicker love-seat, and looks out the door* U. R.)

BRICK. Did you say something?

MARGARET. I was *goin'* t' say somehting: that I get lonely. Very!

BRICK. Ev'rybody gets that.

MARGARET. Living alone with someone you love can be lonelier —than living entirely *alone!*—if the one that y' love doesn't love you.

BRICK. (*Turns to face her.*) Would you like to live alone, Maggie?

MARGARET. (*Turning to him.*) *No! God! I wouldn't!* (*Brick again gestures helplessly. He settles on the couch, whistling, resting his crutch against the* D. S. *side of the wicker seat. He lies with his head* C., *at the foot of the couch, his drink balanced beside him. Margaret crosses toward Brick.*) Did you have a nice shower?

BRICK. Uh-huh.

MARGARET. Was the water cool?

BRICK. No.

MARGARET. But it made you feel fresh, huh?

BRICK. Fresher.

MARGARET. (*Moving to above wicker seat, looking at Brick.*) I know something would make y' feel *much* fresher!

BRICK. What?

MARGARET. An alcohol rub. Or cologne, a rub with cologne!

BRICK. That's good after a work-out, but I haven't been workin'-out, Maggie.

MARGARET. You've kept in good shape, though.

BRICK. You think so, Maggie?

MARGARET. I always thought drinkin' men lost their looks, but I was plainly mistaken.

12

BRICK. Why, thanks, Maggie.

MARGARET. You're the only drinkin' man I know that it never seems t' put fat on.

BRICK. (*Turns on his side, facing* D. S., *away from Margaret.*) I'm gettin' softer, Maggie.

MARGARET. Well, sooner or later it's bound to soften you up. It was just beginning to soften up Skipper when —— (*Margaret stops short and turns away quickly to* C. *Brick sits up, shoots her a look.*) I'm sorry. I never could keep my fingers off a sore. (*Moves* U. S. *at* L. *side of bed.*) I wish you *would* lose your looks. If you did it would make the martyrdom of Saint Maggie a little more bearable. But no such goddam luck. (*She sits on* L. *side of bed.*) I actually believe you've gotten better looking since you've gone on the bottle. A person who didn't know you would think you'd never had a tense nerve in your body or a strained muscle. Of course, you always had that detached quality as if you were playing a game without much concern over whether you won or lost, and now you've lost the game, not lost but just quit playing, you have that rare sort of charm that usually only happens in very old or hopelessly sick people, the charm of the defeated. You look so cool, so cool, so enviably cool. (*Off* U. R., *a croquet game is in progress between Rev. Tooker and Dr. Baugh.* Their conversation, and the click of mallets against croquet balls is partly audible.*)

REV. TOOKER. (*Off* U. R.) Now, looka here, boy —— (*Click of mallet.*) Lemme see you get outa that! (*Margaret rises, crosses above wicker seat to* U. R. *gallery door.*)

MARGARET. They're playing croquet. (*SONG BIRD WHIS-TLES.*) The moon has appeared and it's white, just beginning to turn a little bit yellow. (*Turns to Brick.*) You were a wonderful lover. . . . (*Brick rubs his forehead.*) Such a wonderful person to go to bed with and I think mostly because you were really indifferent to it. Isn't that right? Never had any anxiety about it, did it naturally, easily, slowly, with absolute confidence and perfect calm, more like opening a door for a lady, or seating her at a table, than giving expression to any longing for her. Your indifference made you wonderful at lovemaking. *Strange?* But . . . (*Off* U. R., *the click of mallets.*)

REV. TOOKER. (*Off* U. R.) Oh, that's a beauty!

---

* Baugh is pronounced "Baw."

13

DR. BAUGH. (*Off* U. R.) Yeah, I got you boxed. (*Margaret crosses to* D. R. *corner of bed, sits, facing offstage* R.)

MARGARET. You know, if I thought you would never, never, *never* make love to me again—I would go downstairs to the kitchen and pick out the longest and sharpest knife I could find and stick it straight into my heart. I swear that I would! (*Margaret pantomimes stabbing herself. Off* U. R., *the croquet game continues.*)

REV. TOOKER. (*Off.*) Watch out, now, you gonna miss it.

DR. BAUGH. (*Off.*) You just don' know me, boy!

MARGARET. And later tonight I'm going to tell you I love you an' maybe by that time you'll be drunk enough to believe me. . . . (*Off* U. R., *the click of mallets.*)

REV. TOOKER. (*Off.*) Mmm! You're too slippery for me!

DR. BAUGH. (*Off.*) Jus' like an eel, boy. Jus' like an eel!

MARGARET. (*Rising.*) Yes, they're playing croquet. (*DIS-TANTLY, A HAWK CRIES THREE TIMES. [Sound Cue 1.] Brick looks up intently, listening to the circling hawk. Margaret crosses to wicker chair, sits.*) Big Daddy is dying of cancer. . . . What were you thinkin' of when I caught you looking at me like that? Were you thinking of Skipper? (*Brick takes up his crutch, rises.*) Oh, excuse me, forgive me, but laws of silence don't work. No, laws of silence don't work. (*Brick crosses to bar, takes a quick drink. Margaret, rising, following.*) When something is festering in your memory or your imagination, laws of silence don't work. It's just like shutting a door and locking it on a house on fire in hope of forgetting that the house is burning. But not facing a fire doesn't put it out. (*She crosses to him.*) Silence about a thing just magnifies it. It grows and festers in silence, becomes malignant. . . . (*Margaret puts her hand on Brick's crutch. He pulls away toward* C., *the crutch falls to the floor. Brick circles through* C. *to below the wicker seat, hopping on one foot, holding his glass aloft.*)

BRICK. Give me my crutch.

MARGARET. (*Holding out her arms to Brick.*) Lean on me!

BRICK. No, just give me my crutch.

MARGARET (*Runs to Brick, throws her arms about him.*) Lean on my shoulder!

BRICK. I don't want to lean on your shoulder! (*Violently, Brick, pushes Margaret* U. L. *She turns back to him from below bar.*) I want my crutch. Give me my crutch. Are you going to give me

14

my crutch or do I have to get down on my knees on the floor and ——

MARGARET. (*Runs forward, slides the crutch across to Brick.*) *Here, here, take it, take it!*

BRICK. (*Puts crutch under his arm, hobbles to* D. R. *door.*) Thanks.

MARGARET. (U. C.) That's the first time I've heard you raise your voice in a long time, Brick. A crack in the wall? Of composure?

BRICK. It just hasn't happened yet, Maggie.

MARGARET. What?

BRICK. The click I get in my head when I've had enough of this stuff to make me peaceful. Will you do me a favor?

MARGARET. Maybe I will. What favor?

BRICK. Will you please keep your voice down?

MARGARET. I'll do you that favor. I'll speak in a whisper, if not shut up completely, if *you* will do *me* a favor and make that drink your last one till after the party.

BRICK. What party?

MARGARET. Big Daddy's birthday party.

BRICK. Is this Big Daddy's birthday?

MARGARET. You know this is Big Daddy's birthday!

BRICK. No, I don't, I forgot it.

MARGARET. Well, I remembered it for you. (*Margaret stoops beside the bed,* L. *side, and gets a birthday card in an envelope from beneath the ribbon of a large gift box hidden under the ruffle of the bed.*)

BRICK. Good for you, Maggie.

MARGARET. (*Crosses to night stand for fountain pen.*) You just have to scribble a few lines on this card.

BRICK. (*Crosses* D. S. *onto* D. R. *gallery step.*) You scribble something, Maggie.

MARGARET. It's got to be your handwriting, it's your present, I've given him my present, it's got to be your handwriting!

BRICK. I didn't get him a present.

MARGARET. I got one for you.

BRICK. All right. You write on the card, then.

MARGARET. And have him know that you didn't remember his birthday?

BRICK. I didn't remember his birthday.

15

MARGARET. You don't have to prove you didn't!

BRICK. I don't want to fool him about it. (*Mae Flynn Pollitt appears in the hall, from* L., *bearing the bow from a young lady's archery set. She pauses to listen.*)

MARGARET. (*A step* D. S. *toward Brick.*) Just write "Love, Brick" for God's sake!

BRICK. No.

MARGARET. You've got to!

BRICK. I don't have to do anything I don't want to do. You keep forgetting the conditions on which I agreed to stay on living with you.

MARGARET. I'm not living with you. We occupy the same cage.

BRICK. You've got to remember the conditions agreed on. (*Sonny, one of Mae's children, runs on from* L., *to behind Mae, tries to grab the bow from her and ad libs. a line: "Mommy, give it to me, J had it first!"*)

MARGARET. They're impossible conditions.

BRICK. Then why don't you ——? (*Mae shoos Sonny out* L., *and turns toward the door to the room. Margaret becomes aware of the disturbance in the hall.*)

MARGARET. (*To Brick.*) Hush! (*Turns to door.*) Who is out there? Is somebody at the door? (*Mae pushes open the imaginary hall door, and sweeps past Margaret, crossing to Brick,* D. R. *Sonny sneaks back into the hall, and drops to his hands and knees behind the bar.*)

MAE. (*Holding the bow aloft.*) Brick, is this thing yours? (*Brick sits on the onstage end of the couch.*)

MARGARET. Why, Sister Woman—(*Crosses* D. S. *to* L. *of Mae.*) that's my Diana Trophy. Won it at an intercollegiate archery contest on the Ole Miss campus.

MAE. It's a mighty dangerous thing to leave exposed round a house full of nawmal rid-blooded children attracted t' weapons.

MARGARET. "Nawmal rid-blooded children attracted t' weapons" ought t' be taught to keep their hands off things that don't belong to them.

MAE. (*Embracing Margaret, tentatively.*) Maggie, honey, if you had children of your own you'd know how funny that is. Will you please lock this up and put the key out of reach? (*Hands Margaret the bow.*)

MARGARET. Sister Woman, nobody is plotting the destruction

of your kiddies. (*Sonny creeps around the corner of the bar, R. side, and pokes his head into the room. Mae doesn't see Sonny, since she has turned to the wicker chair to examine the dress Margaret left there.*) Brick and I still have our special archers' license —— (*Crosses to Sonny, kneels beside him.*) We're goin' deer-huntin' on Moon Lake as soon as the season starts. (*Rises.*) I love to run with dogs through chilly woods, run, run, leap over obstructions —— (*She goes into the bathroom, carrying the bow. Sonny rises and runs after Margaret. Mae sees him. Calls out.*)

MAE. Sonny! Go! (*Sonny turns, darts out hall door, and off L.*) How's the injured ankle, Brick?

BRICK. (*Pouring liquor from his drink into the cast.*) Doesn't hurt. Just itches.

MAE. Oh, my! Brick—Brick, you should've been downstairs after supper! Kiddies put on a show! Polly played the piano, Buster an' Sonny drums, an' then they turned out the lights an' Dixie an' Trixie puhfawmed a toe-dance in fairy-costume with *spahklubs!* Big Daddy beamed! He just beamed!

MARGARET. (*From the bathroom, with a sharp laugh.*) Oh, I bet! (*She re-enters, crosses to bed.*) It breaks my heart that we missed it! But, Mae? Why did y' give dawgs' names to all your kiddies? (*Sits on L. side of bed.*)

MAE. *Dawgs'* names?

MARGARET. Dixie an' Trixie an' Buster an' Sonny an' Polly. Sounds t' me like an animal act in a circus. Four dogs and a parrot!

MAE. (*Crosses to below bed, facing Margaret.*) Maggie, honey, why are you so catty?

MARGARET. (*Smiling at Mae.*) Mae, would you know a joke if you bumped into it on Main Street in Memphis at noon?

MAE. *You know* the names of my children! Buster's real name is Robert. Sonny's real name is Saunders. Trixie's real name is Marlene. An' Dixie's is —— (*Gooper, Mae's husband and Brick's brother, appears in the hall from L. He carries a cigarette and a glass of liquor.*)

GOOPER. Hey, Mae! Sister Woman! Intermission's over! (*Off U. L., Sookey and Daisy commence singing.*)

MAE. Intermission is over! See y' later! (*She hurries out the hall door, and off L.*)

GOOPER. (*From the hall, to Brick.*) How's your liquor supply holdin' up, buddy? (*Lifts his glass to Brick, goes out, L.*)

17

MARGARET. I wonder what Dixie's real name is?

BRICK. Maggie—why are you so catty?

MARGARET. I don't know. Why am I so catty? 'Cause I'm consumed with envy and eaten up with longing. (*Rises, crosses to hook on back of bathroom door* D. L. *and gets a silk shirt from the hook.*) Brick, I'm going to lay out your beautiful shantung silk suit from Rome and one of your monogrammed silk shirts. (*Crosses to bed, puts shirt on bed, crosses to night stand and gets out a pair of cuff-links from drawers in night stand.*) I'll put your cuff-links in it, these lovely star sapphires I get you to wear so rarely. (*Kneels at* L. *side bed, starting to put the links in the cuffs of the shirt.*)

BRICK. I can't get trousers on over this plaster cast.

MARGARET. Yes, you can—I'll help you.

BRICK. I'm not going to get dressed, Maggie. (*Pause.*)

MARGARET. Will you just put on a pair of pajamas?

BRICK. Yes, I'll do that, Maggie.

MARGARET. (*Dropping her head momentarily against the shirt.*) Thank you, thank you so much.

BRICK. Don't mention it. (*DISTANTLY, THE HAWK CRIES TWICE. [Sound Cue 2.] Brick looks up, searching for the hawk.*)

MARGARET. (*Rising, runs to Brick, kneels above him.*) Oh, Brick—Brick, how long does it have t' go on? This punishment? Haven't I done time enough? Haven't I served my term? Can't I apply for a—pardon?

BRICK. (*Holding his crutch behind Margaret in his* L. *hand.*) Maggie, lately your voice always sounds like you'd been running upstairs to warn somebody that the house is on fire!

MARGARET. Well, no wonder, no wonder. Y' know what I feel like, Brick? *I feel all the time like a cat on a hot tin roof!* (*Sookey's and Daisy's song stops, off* U. L.)

BRICK. (*Rising.*) Then jump off the roof, jump off it. Cats can jump off roofs and land on their four feet uninjured.

MARGARET. Oh, yes!

BRICK. Do it—fo' God's sake, do it!

MARGARET. Do what?

BRICK. Take a lover.

MARGARET. I can't see a man but you! Even with my eyes closed, I just see you! Why don't you get ugly, Brick, why don't you please get fat or ugly or something so I could stand it? (*She*

18

embraces his legs. Off U. L., *on the words "fat or ugly" in Margaret's above speech, the children commence singing "Jesus Loves Me," with Rev. Tooker punctuating their efforts now and then to utter "Amen!")* Brick—Brick —— *(Looks at him, rises, looks toward the door.)* The concert is still going on! *(Starts toward the door.)* Bravo, no-necks! Bravo! *(She turns her back to the imaginary door, and slams it shut with extended hands—then remains, facing Brick.)* Brick! *(The closing of the imaginary hall door cuts off the song.)*

BRICK. Maggie—what did you lock the door for?

MARGARET. To give us a little privacy for a while.

BRICK. You know better, Maggie.

MARGARET. No, I don't know better.

BRICK. Don't make a fool of yourself.

MARGARET. I don't mind makin' a fool of myself over you!

BRICK. I mind, Maggie. I feel embarrassed for you.

MARGARET. Feel embarrassed! But don't continue my torture. I can't live on and on under these circumstances.

BRICK. You agreed to ——

MARGARET. I know but ——

BRICK. —accept that condition!

BIG MAMA. *(Off* L. *in hall.)* Son! Son! Son!

MARGARET. *(To Brick.)* I CAN'T! I CAN'T! I CAN'T! *(Brick hobbles toward Maggie. Big Mama hurries into the hall, stands above Maggie at the closed door.)*

BIG MAMA. Son!

MARGARET. *(Her back still to the door.)* What is it, Big Mama?

BIG MAMA. Oh, son! We got the most wonderful news about Big Daddy. I just had t' run up an' tell you right this —— *(Notices the locked door.)* What's this door doin' locked faw? You all think there's robbers in the house? *(Brick goes into the bathroom whistling.)*

MARGARET. Big Mama, Brick is dressin', he's not dressed yet.

BIG MAMA. That's all right, it won't be the first time I've seen Brick not dressed. Come on, open this door! *(She crosses* R., *on gallery. Margaret opens the door, looks into the empty hall.)*

MARGARET. Big Mama? *(Big Mama pops in the gallery doors,* U. R., *startling Margaret.)*

BIG MAMA. Where's Brick? *(Attracted by the sound of the whistling, she crosses toward the bathroom door.)* Brick! Hurry on

19

out of there, son, I just have a second and want to give you the news about Big Daddy. (*To Margaret.*) I hate locked doors in a house.

MARGARET. (*Crosses to* L. *side of bed, sits.*) I've noticed you do, Big Mama, but people have got to have *some* moments of privacy, don't they?

BIG MAMA. No, ma'am, not in *my* house! (*Crosses to wicker seat, picks up Margaret's dress.*) Whacha took off that lace dress faw? I thought that little lace dress was so sweet on yuh.

MARGARET. I thought it looked sweet on me, too, but one of m' cute little table-partners used it for a napkin, so ——!

BIG MAMA. So what? (*Crosses* L., *hangs dress on hook behind door* D. L.)

MARGARET. You know, Big Mama, Mae and Gooper's so touchy about those children—thanks, Big Mama—that you just don't dare to suggest there's any room for improvement in their ——

BIG MAMA. (*Calls toward bathroom.*) Brick, hurry out! (*Crosses to Margaret.*) Shoot, Maggie, you just don't like children.

MARGARET. I do SO like children! Adore them!—well brought up . . .

BIG MAMA. (*Gently, loving.*) Well, why don't you have some and bring them up well, then, instead of all the time pickin' on Gooper's an' Mae's?

GOOPER. (*Off* U. R.) Hey! Hey, Big Mama! Betsy an' Hugh got to go! Waitin' t' tell yuh g'by!

BIG MAMA. (*Crosses* R. *to gallery doors, calling off.*) Tell 'em to hold their hawses, I'll be down in a jiffy!

GOOPER. (*Off.*) Yes, ma'am.

BIG MAMA. (*Crosses to bathroom door, calls out.*) Son? Can you hear me in there?

BRICK. (*From bathroom.*) Yes, Big Mama.

BIG MAMA. We just got the full report from the laboratory at the Ochsner Clinic, completely negative, son, ev'rything negative, right on down the line! Nothin' a-tall's wrong with him but some little functional thing—(*Shouting.*) called a spastic colon. Can you hear me, son?

MARGARET. He can hear you, Big Mama.

BIG MAMA. (*To Margaret.*) Then why don't he say somethin'? God A'mighty, a piece of news like that should make him shout. It made *me* shout, I can tell you. I shouted, an' sobbed an' fell right down on my knees! (*Crosses* C.) Look! (*Hoists her skirt to display her knees.*) See the bruises where I hit my knee caps? Took both doctors to haul me back on my feet! (*Laughs, crosses to Margaret, embraces Margaret and starts rubbing Margaret's back, briskly.*) Big Daddy was furious with me! But ain't that wonderful news? After all the anxiety we been through to get a report like that on Big Daddy's birthday? Big Daddy tried to hide how much of a load that news took off his mind, but he didn't fool *me*. He was mighty close to cryin' about it *himself!*

GOOPER. (*Off* U. R.) *Big Mama!* (*PHONE RINGS IN HALL,* L.)

BIG MAMA. (*Calls off* R.) Hold those people down there! Don't let 'em go!

SOOKEY. (*Off* L., *in hall, calls.*) It's Memphis, Miss Ida! It's Miss Sally in Memphis!

BIG MAMA. (*Crosses to hall door.*) I got to go shout at that old deaf fool on the phone. (*Calls off* L.) Aw right, Sookey! (*Calls to bathroom.*) Now get dressed! We're all comin' up to this room fo' Big Daddy's birthday party because of your ankle! (*To Margaret.*) Does it hurt much still?

MARGARET. I'm afraid I can't give you that information, Big Mama. (*Big Mama disappears into the hall. Margaret calls after her.*) You'll have to ask Brick if it hurts much still or not.

BIG MAMA. (*Shouting into the phone, in the hall.*) Hello, Miss Sally! How are you, Miss Sally? (*Brick enters from bathroom, crosses to bar, gets a drink, notices that the bottle is empty. Big Mama, off.*) Yes—well, I was gonna call you about it ——!

MARGARET. (*As Brick tilts the bottle into his glass.*) Brick— don't! (*Brick empties the bottle and tosses it to Margaret. He goes into the bathroom with his drink. Margaret turns on the bed, falls face down across the bed, the bottle beneath her. Throughout this exchange, Big Mama has been screaming into the phone.*)

BIG MAMA. Shoot! Miss Sally, don't ever call me from the Gay-oso Lobby! 'S too much talk goes on in that hotel lobby, no wonder you can't hear me! Now, listen, Miss Sally, we got the report just now! I say there's nothin' serious wrong but a thing called a spastic—*SPAS-TIC*—colon! (*She trots in from the hall.*) Maggie, you come out here an' talk to that fool on the phone! (*Margaret rises, crosses below Big Mama, into hall.*)

MARGARET. (*In the hall, on the phone.*) Miss Sally? This is

Brick's wife, Maggie. So nice to hear your voice—can you hear mine? (*During Margaret's telephone conversation, Big Mama crosses to bed. Sees bottle. Picks it up. Drops it suddenly, as if it had bitten her. Picks it up again, and puts it on the night stand. Picks up Brick's shirt from the bed, crosses to behind wicker seat, puts shirt down across seat. Sees Brick's pillow on the couch,* D. R. *Crosses to couch, looking at it, unhappily. Margaret, continuing on the phone.*) Well, good! Big Mama just wanted you to know that they've got the report from the Ochsner Clinic and what Big Daddy has is a spastic colon. Yes, spastic colon, Miss Sally. G'bye, Miss Sally, hope I'll see you real soon! (*As Margaret re-enters from the hall, Big Mama is picking up Brick's pillow. She holds it tenderly in her arms.*) She heard me perfectly. (*Notices Big Mama with the pillow. Big Mama crosses to bed, puts pillow beside Margaret's on the bed.*)

BIG MAMA. Miss Sally sure is a case!

GOOPER. (*Off* U. R.) Big Mama! Come on now! Betsy an' Hugh cain't wait no longer!

BIG MAMA. (*Shouts over her shoulder.*) I'm comin'! (*Looks at Margaret, points to bottle on night stand.*)

MARGARET. Hmmm?

BIG MAMA. (*Below foot of bed.*) Shoot! Stop playin' so dumb! I mean has he been drinkin' that stuff much yet?

MARGARET. (*Sits on* L. *side of bed, with a little laugh.*) Oh—I think he had a high-ball after supper.

BIG MAMA. Don't laugh about it! Some single men stop drinkin' when they git married and others start! Brick never touched liquor until ——

MARGARET. *THAT'S NOT FAIR!*

BIG MAMA. Fair or not fair, I want to ask you a question, one question: d'you make Brick happy in bed?

MARGARET. Why don't you ask if he makes *me* happy in bed?

BIG MAMA. Because I know that ——

MARGARET. *It works both ways!*

GOOPER. (*Off* U. R.) Come on, Big Mama!

BIG MAMA. Something's not right. You're childless, and my son drinks. (*Points to the bed.*) When a marriage goes on the rocks, the rocks are *here*, right *here*! (*They exchange a look. Big Mama then goes out* U. R. *gallery door, and disappears on the gallery* R., *shaking her head sadly.*)

22

MARGARET. *That's*—not fair. . . . (*Rises, crosses* D. S. *to mirror area, stares at herself.*) Who are you? (*Answering herself, in a small voice.*) I am Maggie the Cat!

BRICK. (*From bathroom.*) Has Big Mama gone?

MARGARET. She's gone. (*Brick appears, crosses to bar, refills glass. Margaret still at mirror.*) You know, our sex life didn't just peter out in the usual way, it was cut off short, long before the natural time for it to, and it's going to revive again, just as sudden as that. I'm confident of it. (*Brick looks around at her. She is aware of his look.*) That's what I'm keeping myself attractive for. For the time when you'll see me again like other men see me. Yes, like other men see me. They still see me, Brick, and they like what they see. (*Brick crosses above to* D. S. *gallery door, carrying his drink.*) Look, Brick! How high my body stays on me!—nothing has fallen on me!—not a fraction! My face looks strained sometimes, but I've kept my figure as well as you've kept yours, and men admire it. I still turn heads on the street. Why, last week in Memphis, everywhere that I went men's eyes burned holes in my clothes, at the country club and in restaurants and department stores, there wasn't a man I met or walked by that didn't just eat me up with his eyes and turn around when I passed him and look back at me. Why, at Alice's party for her New York cousins, the best lookin' man in the crowd followed me upstairs and tried to force his way into the powder room with me, followed me to the door and tried to force his way in! (*During her speech, Brick has seated himself on the* C. *end of the couch.*)

BRICK. Why didn't you let him in, Maggie?

MARGARET. (*Facing him.*) Because I'm not that common, for one thing. Not that I wasn't almost tempted to. You like to know who it was—hmm? (*Her back to audience.*) It was Sonny Boy Maxwell, that's who!

BRICK. Oh, yeah, Sonny Boy Maxwell, he was a good broken-field runner but he had a little injury to his back and had to quit.

MARGARET. (*Circling* U. R. C.) He has no injury now and has no wife and still has a lech for me!

BRICK. I see no reason to lock him out of the powder room in that case. (*Furiously, Maggie grabs the damp bar towel from the bar and flings it at Brick. He catches it effortlessly, and smooths his brow with the cloth. DISTANTLY, THREE HAWK CRIES. [Sound Cue 3.] Margaret stomps into the bathroom. Brick listens*

23

to the birds, following them with his eyes. In a moment, Margaret returns. She has put a negligee over her slip.)

MARGARET. Oh, I might sometime cheat on you with someone, since you're so insultin'ly eager to have me do it!—But if I do, you can be damned sure it will be in a place and at a time where no one but me and the man could possibly know. Because I'm not going to give you any excuse to divorce me for bein' unfaithful or anything else!

BRICK. Maggie, I wouldn't divorce you for bein' unfaithful or anything else. Don't you know that? Hell, I'd be so relieved to know that you'd found yourself a lover.

MARGARET. (L. C.) Well, I'm taking no chances. No, I'd rather stay on this hot tin roof.

BRICK. *(Rising.)* A hot tin roof's 'n uncomfortable place to stay on. *(Starts whistling softly.)*

MARGARET. Yeah, but I can stay on it just as long as I have to.

BRICK. You could leave me, Maggie. *(Whistles.)*

MARGARET. Don't want to and will not! *(Brick turns front in the D. S. door. DISTANTLY 3 HAWK CRIES. [Sound Cue 4.] From R. to L., upstage, Big Daddy strolls across the lawn, followed by Big Mama, who sings to him. He puffs on a big black cigar, and she waves away the tobacco fumes with her handkerchief. Still humming, Big Mama follows Big Daddy off U. L. Margaret crosses to U. S. gallery door at R. To Brick.)* Separation would cost you— *(Crosses to above Brick's shoulder.)* and what have you but what you get from Big Daddy, and he's dyin' of cancer. *(She turns, crosses to U. S. gallery door again.)*

BRICK. *(Sitting on D. S. gallery step.)* Big Mama said he wasn't, that the report was okay.

MARGARET. *(Moving through U. S. door onto gallery and D. R. to R. of Brick.)* That's what she thinks because she got the same story they gave Big Daddy, and was just as taken in by it as he was, poor ole thing. But tonight they're going to tell her the truth about it. When Big Daddy goes to bed, they're going to tell her that he's dying of cancer. It's malignant and it's hopeless.

BRICK. Does Big Daddy know it?

MARGARET. *(Crouching at R. of Brick.)* Hell, do they *ever* know it? Nobody says, "You're dying." You have to fool them. They have to fool *themselves. (DISTANTLY 3 HAWK CRIES.) [Sound Cue 5.]* So this is Big Daddy's last birthday, and do you know something, Brick? Big Daddy's made no will. Big Daddy never made out any will in his life, and that's why Mae and Gooper have launched their campaign to impress him as forcibly as they can with the fact that you drink, and I've borne no children. (*DIS-TANTLY, 2 HAWK CRIES. [Sound Cue 6.] Brick whistles after the hawks.*) Oh, Brick, Brick, y'know, I've been so goddam disgustingly poor all my life! That's the *truth*, Brick!

BRICK. I'm not sayin' it isn't.

MARGARET. Always had to suck up to people I couldn't stand because they had money and I was poor as Job's turkey. You don't know what that's like. Well, I'll tell you, it's like you would feel a thousand miles away from Echo Spring—and you had to get back to it on that broken ankle—without a crutch! That's how it feels to be as poor as Job's turkey and have to suck up to relatives that you hated because they had money and all you had was a bunch of hand-me-down clothes and a few old mouldy three percent government bonds. My daddy loved his liquor, he fell in love with his liquor like you've fallen in love with Echo Spring! And my poor Mama, havin' to maintain some semblance of social position to keep appearances up, on an income of one hundred and fifty dollars a month on those old government bonds! When I came out, the year that I made my debut, I had just two evening dresses —one my mother made me from a pattern in *Vogue*, the other a hand-me-down from a snotty rich cousin I hated. The dress that I married you in was my grandmother's wedding gown! (*DIS-TANTLY, 2 HAWK CRIES.*) [Sound Cue 7.] You can be young without money but you can't be old without it. You've got to be old *with* money because to be old without it is just too awful, you've got to be one or the other, either *young* or *with money*, you can't be old and *without* it. That's the truth, Brick. (*FROG NOISES OFF* R. *[Sound Cue 8.] Brick rises, crosses to bar.*) Well, now, I'm dressed. I'm all dressed and there's nothing else for me to do. I'm dressed, all dressed, nothing else for me to do. (*Brick opens bottle at bar, pours drink.*) I know where I made my mistake. I've thought a whole lot about it and now I know when I made my mistake. Yes, I made my mistake when I told you the truth about that thing with Skipper. (*Brick turns toward her.*) Never should have confessed it, a fatal error tellin' you about that thing with Skipper.

BRICK. Maggie, shut up about Skipper. I mean it, Maggie, you got to shut up about Skipper.

MARGARET. (*Turning to him from the step.*) You ought to understand that Skipper and I ——

BRICK. You don't think I'm serious, Maggie? You're fooled by the fact that I am sayin' this quiet? (*Crosses toward her with drink.*) Look, Maggie, what you're doin' is a dangerous thing to do. You're—you're—you're foolin' with somethin' that nobody ought to fool with!

MARGARET. (*Looking up at him, where he stands, R. C.*) This time I'm going to finish what I have to say to you—you superior creature—you god-like being! Yes! Truth, truth! What's so awful about it? I like it. I think the truth is —— (*Turns away.*)

BRICK. It was Skipper that told me about it. Not you, Maggie.

MARGARET. I told you! (*From U. R. to U. L., Dixie rushes across the lawn, followed rapidly by Trixie. Dixie shouts "I got your mallet!" and brandishes a croquet mallet. Trixie screams for the mallet's return. They disappear U. L.*)

BRICK. (*Crosses R. to U. R. step.*) After he told me!

MARGARET. What does it matter who ——?

BRICK. (*Crosses onto upper gallery, calling after the children.*) Little girl! Hey, little girl! Tell the folks to come up! Bring everybody upstairs! (*Speeches overlapping.*)

MARGARET. I can't stop myself! I'd go on telling you this in front of them all, if I had to!

BRICK. Little girl! Go on, go on, will you? Do what I told you! You bring everybody up here!

MARGARET. Because it's got to be told and you, you—you never let me! (*Pause.*) You had one of those beautiful ideal things they tell about in the Greek legends, it couldn't be anything else, you being you, and that's what made it so sad, that's what made it so awful, because it was love that never could be carried through to anything satisfying or even talked about plainly.

BRICK. (*Crosses to above wicker seat.*) Maggie, you got to stop this!

MARGARET. Brick, I tell you, you got to believe me, Brick. I *do* understand all about it! I—I think it was—*noble!* Can't you tell I'm sincere when I say I respect it? My only point, the only point that I'm makin', is life has got to be allowed to continue even

26

after the *dream* of life is—all over. (*Brick puts his drink in the wicker seat, rests his crutch across the back of the seat.*)

BRICK. Maggie, you want me to hit you with this crutch? Don't you know that I could kill you with this crutch?

MARGARET. Good Lord, man, d'you think I'd care if you did?

BRICK. One man has one great good true thing in his life. One great good thing which is true! I had friendship with Skipper. You are namin' it dirty!

MARGARET. I'm not namin' it dirty! I am namin' it clean!

BRICK. Not love with you, Maggie, but friendship with Skipper, and you are namin' it dirty!

MARGARET. Then you haven't been listenin', not understood what I'm sayin'! I'm namin' it so damn clean that it killed poor Skipper! You two had somethin' that had to be kept on ice, yes, incorruptible, yes! and death was the only icebox where you could keep it!

BRICK. I married you, Maggie. Why would I marry you, Maggie —(*Lifts crutch warningly.*) if I was ——?

MARGARET. Brick, don't! Let me finish! I know, believe me, I know that it was only Skipper that harbored even any *unconscious* desire for anything not perfectly pure between you two! (*Brick turns* u. s., *rests crutch on bed, his hands clenched around the shaft of the crutch.*) You married me early that summer we graduated out of Ole Miss, and we were happy, weren't we, we were blissful, yes, hit heaven together ev'ry time that we loved! But that Fall you an' Skipper turned down wonderful offers of jobs in order to keep on bein' football heroes—pro-football heroes. You organized the Dixie Stars that Fall so you could keep on bein' team-mates forever! But somethin' was not right with it!—*Me included!*—between you. Skipper began hittin' the bottle . . . you got a spinal injury—couldn't play the Thanksgivin' game in Chicago, watched it on TV from a traction bed in Toledo. I joined Skipper. The Dixie Stars lost because poor Skipper was drunk. We drank together that night all night in the bar of the Blackstone and when cold day was comin' up over the Lake an' we were comin' out drunk to take a dizzy look at it, I said, "SKIPPER! STOP LOVIN' MY HUSBAND OR TELL HIM HE'S GOT TO LET YOU ADMIT IT TO HIM!"—one way or another! (*Brick strikes the bed, ominously, with his crutch.*) *He slapped me hard in the mouth!*—then turned and ran without stoppin' once, all the

27

way back to his room at the Blackstone. That night, when I came to his room that night, with a little scratch, like a shy little mouse at the door, he made that pitiful, ineffectual little attempt to prove that what I had said wasn't true. (*Brick charges* D. S. *at Maggie with the blunt end of the crutch directed at her. She cries out, leaps up, and runs* U. R. *onto upper gallery and into the room through the* U. R. *doors. He turns on the* D. S. *gallery, leaning on his crutch, staring at her through the* D. S. *door.*) No, no, no! (*Faces him,* R. C., *in the room.*) In this way, I destroyed him, by telling him truth that his world which he was born and raised in, had taught him couldn't be told! From then on Skipper was nothin' at all but a receptacle for liquor an' drugs. *Who shot Cock Robin? I—with my merciful arrow!* (*Brick hobbles toward Margaret, his crutch still wrong-end-up. He moves through the room,* D. S. C., *as she circles away from him, backing toward the bar.*) Brick, Brick, I'm not tryin' to whitewash my behavior, Christ, no! Brick, I'm not good. I don't know why people have to pretend to be good, nobody's good. The rich or the well-to-do can afford to respect moral patterns, conventional moral patterns, but I never could afford to, yeah, but I'm honest! Give me credit for just that, will you, *please?* Born poor, raised poor, expect to die poor unless I can manage to get us something out of what Big Daddy leaves when he dies of cancer! But, Brick! *Skipper is dead! I'm alive!* Maggie the Cat is alive! *I'm alive, alive!* (*Brick strikes at Margaret, swinging the crutch like a baseball bat. She ducks beside the bar. The crutch slips from Brick's grasp and falls,* R. C. *Brick sinks to the floor,* D. S. C. *At the same moment, Buster, Sonny, Dixie and Trixie rush into the room, firing cap pistols, and screaming "Bang! Bang! Bang!" Buster runs into the room through the hall door, and stands above Brick, emptying the cap pistol at Brick. The others enter the room after they have raced across the upper gallery to the* U. R. *doors. They arrange themselves behind and below the wicker seat.*) Little children, your mother or someone should teach you to knock at a door before you come into a room, otherwise people might think that you lack good breedin'.

BUSTER. What's Uncle Brick doin' on the floor?

BRICK. I tried to kill your Aunt Maggie, but I failed, and I fell.

MARGARET. Give your uncle his crutch, he's a cripple, honey. (*Buster crosses* R. C., *gets crutch, hands it to Brick.*) He broke his ankle last night jumpin' hurdles on the high school athletic field.

28

BUSTER. Why were you jumpin' hurdles, Uncle Brick?

BRICK. Because I used to jump them, an' people like t' do what they used t' do, even after they've stopped bein' able t' do it.

MARGARET. That's right, that's your answer—now go away! (*On "that's your answer" in the above line, the children charge across the room, firing their cap pistols point blank at Margaret, who covers her face with her hands.*) Stop! You stop that—you monsters! (*Trixie, Sonny and Buster race out through the hall door, shouting "Bang! Bang! Bang!" and firing their pistols until they are out of sight. Dixie pauses by the R. end of the bar, facing Margaret.*)

DIXIE. You're *jealous*. You're just jealous because you can't have babies! (*She grins at Margaret, and with a simpering look over her shoulder, goes out through the hall and off L. Brick rises, hobbles D. R. toward foot of couch. Margaret laughs.*)

MARGARET. You see? They gloat over us bein' childless, even in front of their no-neck monsters! (*A step C.*) Brick, I've been to a doctor in Memphis. I've been examined, an' there's no reason why we can't have a child whenever we want one. Are you listenin' to me? Are you? Are you LISTENIN' TO ME?

BRICK. (*He has picked up his glass from the wicker seat.*) Yes, I hear you, Maggie, but how in hell on earth do you imagine that you're going to have a child by a man that can't stand you?

MARGARET. That's a problem that I will have to work out. (*There is the sound of adult voices approaching in the hall from L. Margaret wheels to face the hall door.*) Here they come! (*THE LIGHTS DIM OUT.*)

CURTAIN

ACT II

The action continues.

Margaret and Brick are in the same positions they held at the end of Act I: she is facing the hall, U. C., just below the R. side of the hall door; he is D. S., at the L. end of the couch, holding his drink. THE LIGHTS BUILD.

MARGARET. Here they come! (*Big Daddy enters from the hall. Margaret stops him as he enters the room, and gives him a kiss. Big Daddy moves D. R. C. toward Brick. Margaret crosses to bar.*)
BIG DADDY. Hello, Brick. (*At this point, Gooper and Rev. Tooker enter through the hall, cross R. through upper gallery. The dialogue overlaps.*)

BRICK. Hello, Big Daddy. Congratulations. (*Lifts glass.*)
BIG DADDY. Crap! (*Big Daddy turns R., sees Gooper and Rev. Tooker entering doors U. R., turns back to hall, just as Mae and Dr. Baugh enter from the hall. He is trapped U. R. C.*)
MAE. (*To Dr. Baugh.*) Let's see now, they've had their typhoid shots, an' their tetanus shots, their diphtheria shots an' their hepatitis shots an' their polio shots —— (*Mae leads Dr. Baugh D. L. C.*)
MAE. Gooper! Hey, Gooper! What all have the kiddies been shot fo'?

GOOPER. I read in the Register that you're gettin' a new memorial window.
REV. TOOKER. Isn't that nice, but St. Paul's in Grenada has three memorial windows, an' th' latest one is a Tiffany stain' glass window that cost $2500, a picture of Christ—the Good Shepherd with a lamb in his arms.
GOOPER. Who give that window, Preach?
REV. TOOKER. Clyde Fletcher's widow. Also presented St. Paul's with a baptismal font.
GOOPER. Y' know, what somebody oughta give your church is a coolin' system, Preach.
REV. TOOKER. Yessiree, bob!

30

GOOPER. Everything but stealin' chickens, I guess! (*General laugh. Brick has crossed onto lower gallery.*)

MAE. (*To Dr. Baugh.*) They get those shots ev'ry month, May through September.

REV. TOOKER. (*To Gooper.*) An' y' know what Gus Hanna's fam'ly gave in his mem'ry t' th' Church at Two Rivers? A complete new stone parish house with a basketball court in the basement an' ——

BIG DADDY. Hey, Preach! What's all this talk about memorials, Preach? Y' think somebody's about t' kick off around here? 'S that it?

MARGARET. Turn on the Hi-Fi, Brick. Let's have some music t' start th' party with. (*Crosses D. R. toward Brick.*)

BRICK. You turn it on.

MARGARET. (*By foot of couch.*) I don't know how to turn it on.

(*Mae starts for the radio controls at the L. end of the bar.*)

GOOPER. We gave 'em that thing for a third anniversary present, got three speakers in it.

(*Mae turns on the radio. Dial lights up. A loud, unctuous "political" voice booms from the amplifier.*)

VOICE. [*Sound Cue 9.*] Th' disgustin' mendacity which my opponent has shown ——

BIG DADDY. Turn that thing off! (*Mae turns off the radio. Big Mama charges in from the hall.*)

BIG MAMA. *Wha's mah Brick? Wha's mah precious baby!!*

BIG DADDY. *Sorry! Turn it back on!* (*Mae turns another knob. The dial lights and the TV screen flickers at the R. end of the bar. Gooper and Rev. Tooker look at the TV. Mae and Dr. Baugh remain D. L. C. Margaret sits on the U. S. side of the couch. Big Daddy sinks into the wicker seat.*)

BIG MAMA. (*Crosses D. R. and onto lower gallery to Brick.*) Here he is, here's mah precious baby! What's that you got in your hand? Yo' hand was made fo' holdin' somethin' better'n that! You put that liquor down, son! (*Brick drinks.*)

GOOPER. (*Turning D. C., and peering out the D. S. door.*) Look at ole Brick put it down! (*He turns, laughing, to Mae and Dr.*

31

Baugh. Rev. Tooker crosses to above wicker seat. He looks at the TV with Gooper and Dr. Baugh.)

BIG MAMA. Oh, you bad boy, you're my bad little boy. Give Big Mama a kiss, you bad boy, you! Look at him shy away, will yuh? Brick never liked bein' kissed or made a fuss ovah, I guess because he's always had too much of it ——

VOICE. (From TV amplifier.) [Sound Cue 10.] —there's a man on second—and there's the pitch ——!

BIG MAMA. (Turning U. C. into room.) You turn that thing off! (Mae crosses to controls, turns off set. She drifts D. L. C., joined by Gooper and Dr. Baugh, and Rev. Tooker.) I can't stand TV, radio was bad enough, but TV has gone it one better—I mean, one worse! (Plops herself onto the D. S. corner of the bed.) Now, what am I sittin' here faw? I want to sit nex' to mah sweetheart, hold hands with him, an' love him up a little! (Rises, tries to get into seat beside Big Daddy.) Move over! (She cannot budge Big Daddy.) Just like Brick! (Big Daddy grunts, rises, gives Big Mama the seat. She flops into it. Big Daddy crosses D. R. to the lower gallery door. To Rev. Tooker.) Preacher, Preacher, hey, Preach! Give me yo' hand an' he'p me up from this chair!

REV. TOOKER. (Crosses to her.) None of your tricks, Big Mama!

BIG MAMA. What tricks? You give me yo' hand so I can git up an' —— (Rev. Tooker gives Big Mama his hand. She pulls him down into her lap, and chants, as she bounces him up and down, to general laughter.) Ever see a preacher in a lady's lap? Hey, folks! Ever see a preacher in a lady's lap? (Sookey enters from hall with a message for Mae. She whispers to Mae, and Mae and Sookey go out through the hall door. Laughing at Big Mama, Gooper and Dr. Baugh drop a bit more D. L.)

BIG DADDY. (Yelling at Big Mama.) BIG MAMA, WILL YOU QUIT HORSIN'?

BIG MAMA. Get up, Preacher. (Rev. Tooker rises, with some difficulty. He crosses to above wicker seat, smoothing his clothes.)

BIG DADDY. (To Big Mama.) You're courtin' a stroke! (Off L., in the hall, a pitch-pipe cues children to start singing "Happy Birthday.")

HAPPY BIRTHDAY

(Sung by Mae, the Children, and Field Hands. Cue: Big Daddy: Big Mama, will you quit horsin'? You're courtin' a stroke. Mae

32

starts song off L. *in hall, leads Children on. Field Hands enter* R.
on lawn, singing.)
Happy birthday to you.
Happy birthday to you.
Happy birthday, Big Daddy.
(*Field Hands: Dear Cap'n! How old are you?*)
(*Field Hands ad lib. birthday greetings and blessings. Mae crosses
down, faces Children front and begins.*)
Skinamarinka—dinka—dink
Skinamarinka—do
We love you.
Skinamarinka—dinka—dink
Skinamarinka—do (*They turn to Big Daddy.*)
Big Daddy, you! (*They turn front.*)
We love you in the morning
We love you in the night.
We love you when we're with you,
And we love you out of sight.
Skinamarinka—dinka—dink
Skinamarinka—do. (*Mae turns to Big Mama.*)
Big Mama, too! (*Big Mama turns down, cries. Dialogue resumes.*)
BIG DADDY. Now, Ida, what the hell is the matter with you?
BIG MAMA. (*Hurrying through* C. *to* D. L.) *Here comes Big
Daddy's birthday!* (*The singing swells. Off* U. R., *a field bell starts
ringing.* [*Sound Cue 11.*] *Daisy, Brightie, Small and Lacey appear
in the* U. R. *lawn area singing "Happy Birthday" as a procession
enters from the hall. Trixie comes first, carrying a huge, candle-
laden cake, ablaze. She is followed by Sonny, Buster and Dixie, all
in fancy paper hats. Mae brings up the rear. Sookey moves into the
hall. Daisy leaves the singers in the yard, and enters along a gallery
to* U. S. *near the hall door. Big Daddy, attracted by the singers in
the yard, moves* R. *to* U. R. *gallery doors, waves to the field hands.
At the end of "Happy Birthday," the field hands depart, except for
Brightie and Small. The bell stops ringing.* [*End of Sound Cue 11.*]
Mae swoops D. C., *arranging the children in a line, facing front.
She cues them into the song, "Skinamarink-a-doo." Rev. Tooker
takes the cake from Trixie, passes the cake to Sookey,* U. C., *who
puts it on the* R. *end of the bar, then stands in the hall door, beam-
ing. When the children salute Big Daddy in their song, he lets out
a cry.*)

33

BIG DADDY. (*Turning away to* R.) Je-sus! (*Brightie and Small leave the yard. At the end of their song, the children salute Big Mama. She bursts into tears. Mae hurries to her, D. L.*) Ida, what the hell's the matter with you?

MAE. She's just so happy!

BIG MAMA. I'm just so happy, Big Daddy, I have to cry, or somethin'! (*Pushes Mae away and crosses D. R. onto gallery to Brick. Sonny and Buster cross to above and below Mae, who is joined by Gooper, D. L. C. Dixie crosses to bar and scrapes sugar off the cake. Trixie holds, U. R. C., watching Big Daddy.*) Brick, do you know the wonderful news Doc Baugh got from th' clinic about Big Daddy? Big Daddy's one hundred percent!

MARGARET. Isn't that wonderful?

BIG MAMA. He's just one hundred percent. Passed the examination with flyin' colors. Now that we know there's nothin' wrong with Big Daddy but a spastic colon, I can tell you somethin'. I was worried sick, half out of my mind, fo' fear that Big Daddy might have a thing like ——

MARGARET. (*Quickly, rising, and crosses to L. of bed.*) Brick, honey, aren't you going to give Big Daddy his birthday present? (*Gets package out from beneath bed, puts it on bed, sits.*) Here it is, Big Daddy, this is from Brick! (*The children shriek, and race to the bed, throwing themselves on the gift box. Sookey, Rev. Tooker and Mae shoo them out. Big Mama crosses to R. of Margaret below bed, picks up birthday card. Daisy and Sookey vanish with the children into the hall.*)

BIG MAMA. This is the biggest birthday Big Daddy's ever had, a hundred presents and bushels of telegrams from —— (*Looks toward Brick.*) What is it, Brick? (*Mae remains standing at L. of Margaret, who is still seated on bed. Gooper at C.*)

GOOPER. (*Crosses D. S., looking out at Brick.*) I bet 500 to 50 Brick doesn't know what it is.

BIG MAMA. The fun of presents is not knowin' what they are till you open the package. Open your present, Big Daddy. (*After he has helped chase the kids away, Rev. Tooker has joined Dr. Baugh, D. L. Gooper now drifts up to the bar, lights a cigarette, gets a drink. Big Daddy crosses to lower gallery door.*)

BIG DADDY. Open it you'self. I want to ask Brick somethin'. Come here, Brick.

BIG MAMA. (*Crosses to bed.*) Open it! Open it!

34

GOOPER. Big Daddy's callin' you, Brick.

BRICK. Tell Big Daddy I'm crippled.

BIG DADDY. I see you're crippled. I want to know how you got crippled.

MARGARET. (*Removing the gift from the box.*) Oh, look, oh, look, why, it's a cashmere robe. (*Holds the robe up for all to see.*)

MAE. You sound surprised, Maggie.

MARGARET. I never saw one before.

MAE. That's funny—*HAH!*

MARGARET. Why is it funny?

BIG DADDY. (*Ominously.*) Quiet!

BRICK. (*An echo.*) Quiet!

MAE. (*To Margaret.*) You bought it yourself at Lowenstein's in Memphis last Saturday. You know how I know?

BIG DADDY. I said "Quiet"!

BRICK. (*Softly.*) Quiet!

MAE. I know because the salesgirl that sold it to you waited on me an' said, "Oh, Mrs. Pollitt, your sister-in-law just bought a cashmere robe for your husband's father!" (*Big Mama tiptoes through gallery doors U. R. to lower gallery, carrying the birthday card to Brick. She comes to L. of Brick, tries to attract his attention.*)

MARGARET. Sister Woman ——!

BIG DADDY. QUIET!   BRICK. Quiet. . . .

REV. TOOKER. (*To Dr. Baugh, D. L., finishing a sentence.*) —the stork and the Reaper are runnin' neck an' neck! (*Sudden silence.*)

BIG DADDY. Preacher, I hope I'm not buttin' in on more talk about memorial stained glass windows, am I, Preacher? (*Margaret puts the robe back into the box. Mae lifts her arms and jangles her bracelets.*)

MAE. (*To Rev. Tooker, starting D. L.*) I wonder if the mosquitoes are active tonight?

BIG DADDY. What's that, Little Mama? Did you make some remark?

MAE. (*At L. with Rev. Tooker, Gooper, Dr. Baugh.*) Yes, I said I wondered if the mosquitoes would eat us alive if we went out on th' gallery ——

BIG DADDY. Well, if they do, I'll have your bones pulverized for fertilizer!

BIG MAMA. Last week we had an airplane sprayin' th' place an' I think it done some good, at least I haven't had a —— (*Brick slaps at a mosquito.*)

BIG DADDY. Brick, they tell me, if what they tell me is true, that you done some jumpin' last night on the high school athletic field?

BIG MAMA. (*Closer to Brick, at his* L.) Brick, Big Daddy is talkin' to you, son.

BRICK. (*Crosses below Big Mama toward Big Daddy.*) What was that, Big Daddy?

BIG DADDY. They say you done some jumpin' on the high school track field last night.

BRICK. That's what they told me, too.

BIG DADDY. Was it jumpin' or *bumpin'* that you were doin' out there?

BIG MAMA. Oh, Big Daddy! (*Laughs, a little embarrassed.*)

BIG DADDY. What were you doin' out there at three a.m.? (*Mae crosses protectively toward Rev. Tooker.*)

BIG MAMA. (*Crosses above Brick to* R. *of Big Daddy—she is still on the lower gallery, Big Daddy on the step, in the room.*) Big Daddy, you are off the sick-list now an' I'm not goin' to excuse you for talkin' ——

BIG DADDY. Quiet!

BIG MAMA. —so nasty ——

BIG DADDY. Be quiet!

BIG MAMA. In front of Preacher an' ——

BIG DADDY. QUIET! (*Big Mama crosses to* D. R. *gallery door, enters, and crosses to below Margaret at foot of bed.*) I ast you, Brick, if you was cuttin' yourself a piece o' poon-tang last night on that cinder track? (*Gooper laughs, Mae is torn between shushing him and trying to divert Rev. Tooker's attention.*) I thought maybe you were chasin' some wild poon-tang ——

MAE. (*Drawing the Preacher out through hall door.*) Reverend Tooker, let's you an' I take a stroll along th' gallery.

BIG DADDY. G'by, Preacher. (*To Brick.*) —on that track—an' tripped over somethin' in th' heat of th' chase . . . is that it? (*Gooper laughs, puts down a drink at bar.*)

BRICK. No, sir, I don't think so. (*Gooper starts out through the* R. *gallery, via the hall door, following Mae and Rev. Tooker, who have vanished along* R. *gallery, and out. Dr. Baugh is still* D. L.

36

Big Mama draws Margaret from the bed to the bar, and they put their heads together. Margaret pours a drink.)

BIG DADDY. Then what th' hell were you doin' out there at three o'clock in th' mornin'?

BRICK. Jumpin' the hurdles, Big Daddy, runnin' an' jumpin' the hurdles, but those high hurdles have gotten too high for me now.

BIG DADDY. 'Cause you were drunk?

BRICK. Sober, I wouldn't have tried to jump the *low* ones.

BIG MAMA. (*Carries birthday cake* D. R. C.) Big Daddy, come blow out th' candles on your birthday cake!

MARGARET. (*Crosses* D. R. C. *to Big Daddy, who turns to her.*) I want to propose a toast to Big Daddy Pollitt on his sixty-fifth birthday, the biggest cotton-planter in —— (*Dr. Baugh turns to the bar, drinks.*)

BIG DADDY. *I told you to stop it, now stop it, quit this bull!* (*Margaret crosses above Big Daddy to* U. R. *gallery door, out onto gallery, and around* D. R. *to Brick, handing him her glass.*)

BIG MAMA. (*Crosses to Big Daddy with cake.*) Big Daddy, I will not allow you to talk that way, not even on your birthday. I ——

BIG DADDY. I'll talk like I want to on my birthday, Ida, or any goddam day of the year an' anybody here that don't like it knows what they can do!

BIG MAMA. You don't mean that!

BIG DADDY. What makes you think I don't mean it!

BIG MAMA. I just know you don't mean it.

BIG DADDY. You don't know a goddam thing an' you never did!

BIG MAMA. Big Daddy, you don't mean that.

BIG DADDY. Oh, yes, I do, oh, yes, I do mean it! I put up with a whole lot of crap around here because I thought I was dyin' —— (*Crosses above Big Mama to* L. C.) An' you thought I was dyin' an' you started takin' over; well, you can stop takin' over, now, Ida, because I'm not goin' to die, you can just stop this business of takin' over because you're not takin' over because I'm not dyin'. I went through that laboratory and the exploratory operation and there's nothin' wrong with me but a spastic colon. An' I'm not dyin' of cancer which you thought I was dyin' of. (*Dr. Baugh takes his glass and goes out through hall door and exits along* R. *gallery. Big Daddy has crossed during speech [on the word "laboratory"] to* R. *of Big Mama. Continuing his tirade to Big Mama.*)

Ain't that so? Didn't you think that I was dyin' of cancer? Ain't that so, Ida? Didn't you have an idea I was dyin' of cancer an' now you could take control of this place an' everything on it? I got that impression, I seemed to get that impression. Your loud voice everywhere, your damn' busy ole body buttin' in here an' there! (*Mae and Rev. Tooker have started in along* R. *gallery toward* U. R. *doors.*)

BIG MAMA. Hush! The Preacher!

BIG DADDY. Rut the Preacher! Did you hear what I said? Rut the cotton-pickin', chicken-eatin', memorial-stained-glass Preacher! (*Mae skillfully turns the Preacher at the doors,* U. R., *and leads him off, once again, out* R., *along gallery.*)

BIG MAMA. I never seen you act like this before an' I can't think what's got into you!

BIG DADDY. I went through all that laboratory an' operation an' all just so I would know if you or me was boss here! Well, now it turns out that I am an' you ain't—and that's my birthday present —an' my cake an' champagne—because for three years now you been gradually takin' over. Bossin', talkin', sashayin' your ole butt aroun' this place I made! I made this place! (*Crosses* D. S., *speaks directly to audience.*) I was overseer on it! I was the overseer on th' ole Straw an' Ochello plantation. I quit school at ten! I quit school at ten years old an' went to work like a nigger in th' fields. An' I rose to be overseer of th' Straw an' Ochello plantation. An' ole Straw died an' I was Ochello's partner an' the place got bigger an' bigger an' bigger an' bigger! I did all that myself with no goddam help from you, an' now you think that you're just about to take over. Well, I'm just about to tell you that you are not just about to take over, you are not just about to take over a goddam thing. Is that clear to you, Ida? Is that very plain to you now? Is that understood completely? I been through the laboratory from A to Z. (*Crosses* R. *above Big Mama to her* R.) I've had the goddam exploratory operation, an' nothin' is wrong with me but a spastic colon—made spastic, I guess, by all th' goddam lies an' liars that I have had to put up with, an' all th' hypocrisy that I have lived with all these forty years that I been livin' with you! Now, blow out the candles on th' birthday cake! Take a deep breath an' blow out th' goddam candles on th' cake!

BIG MAMA. Oh, Big Daddy, in all these years you never believed that I loved you ——

38

BIG DADDY. Huh!

BIG MAMA. And I did, I did so much. I did love you. I even loved your hate an' your hardness, Big Daddy! (*Off* u. r., *the field hands commence singing. Big Mama, fighting her tears, takes the cake out through the* u. r. *doors and out the* r. *gallery exit.*)

BIG DADDY. (*To himself.*) Wouldn't it be funny if that was true? (*Turns to* d. s. *gallery door.*) BRICK! HEY, BRICK! (*Margaret steps to the door on the* d. s. *gallery.*) I didn't call you, Maggie. I called Brick.

MARGARET. I'm just deliverin' him to you. (*Margaret draws Brick toward the door. She kisses him, then she goes out above couch, through* u. r. *gallery doors, and exits along gallery* r. *Brick wipes Margaret's kiss from his lips, as he stands by the foot of the couch.*)

BIG DADDY. Why did you do that?

BRICK. Do what, Big Daddy?

BIG DADDY. Wipe her kiss off your mouth?

BRICK. I don't know, I wasn't conscious of it.

BIG DADDY. That woman of yours has a better shape on her than Gooper's got on his woman. (*SONG FADES OFF, AT* u. r.)

BRICK. 'Sthat all the difference you notice?

BIG DADDY. Diff'rences in shape is pretty important.

BRICK. But don't you think they's a fundamental resemblance, I mean like between a couple of Plymouth Rocks or Rhode Island Reds?

BIG DADDY. Sure, sure—but it's funny.

BRICK. What's funny?

BIG DADDY. That you an' Gooper, in spite of bein' so diff'rent, would pick out more or less the same type of woman.

BRICK. We married into society, Big Daddy.

BIG DADDY. Why do both of 'em have that same anxious look?

BRICK. Well, they're sittin' in th' middle of a big piece of land, Big Daddy, twenty-eight thousand acres is a pretty big piece of land an' so they're squarin' off on it, each determined to knock off a bigger piece of it than th' other whenever you let it go. (*Mae has re-appeared on the gallery* r., *and moves* u. s. *along gallery, listening.*)

BIG DADDY. I got a surprise for those women. I'm not goin' to let it go for a long time yet, if that's what they're waitin' for.

BRICK. That's right, Big Daddy. You just sit tight an' let 'em scratch each other's eyes out.

BIG DADDY. You bet your life I'm goin' to sit tight on it an' let 'em scratch their eyes out. But Gooper's wife is a good breeder, you got to admit she's fertile. Hell, at supper tonight she had 'em all at the table an' they had to put in a couple of extra leaves in the table to make room for 'em, she's got five head of 'em now, an' another one's comin'.

BRICK. Yep, number six is comin'.

BIG DADDY. Six, hell, she'll probably drop a litter next time!

GOOPER. (*Off* U. R.) *MAE! HEY, MAE!* (*Mae, hiding on the upper gallery, tries to shush Gooper.*)

BIG DADDY. Somebody out there? (*To Brick.*) Gooper? (*Calls.*)

GOOPER! (*Mae bursts into the room from* U. R. *gallery entrance, crosses to* L. *of Big Daddy.*)

MAE. Do you want Gooper, Big Daddy?

BIG DADDY. No, I don't want Gooper an' I don't want you! (*He backs her* U. S. *to hall door.*) I want some privacy here while I'm havin' a confidential talk with my son Brick. Now it's too hot in here to close them doors, but if I have to close them ruttin' doors in order to have a private talk with my son Brick, just let me know an' I'll close 'em. Because I hate eavesdroppers. I don't like any kind of sneakin' an' spyin' ——

MAE. Why, Big Daddy, I didn't ——

BIG DADDY. You stood on the wrong side of the moon, it threw your shadow!

MAE. I was just ——

BIG DADDY. You was just nothin' but *spyin'* an' you *know* it!

MAE. (*With a sniff and a sob.*) Oh, Big Daddy, you're so unkind for some reason to those that really love you!! (*Big Daddy uses his next speech to back Mae along gallery* R. *toward the gallery exit,* R.)

BIG DADDY. Shut up, shut up, shut up! I'm goin' to move you an' Gooper out of that room next to this!! It's none of your goddam business what goes on here at night between Brick an' Maggie. You listen at night like a couple of ruttin' peek-hole spies, an' go an' give a report on what you hear to Big Mama an' she comes to me an' says they say such an' such an' so an' so about what they heard goin' on between Brick an' Maggie, an' Jesus, it makes me sick! I'm goin' to move you an' Gooper out of that room. I can't

40

stand sneakin' an' spyin', it makes me *puke!* (*Brick has gone to the bar during the above speech. Now, Big Daddy re-enters the room through the u. r. gallery doors.*)

BRICK. They listen, do they?

BIG DADDY. (*Crosses* c.) Yeah, they listen an' give reports to Big Mama on what goes on here between you an' Maggie. They say that you won't sleep with her, that you sleep on the sofa. Is that true or not true? If you don't like Maggie, get rid of Maggie! What are you doin' there now?

BRICK. Fresh'nin' up my drink.

BIG DADDY. Son, you know you got a real liquor problem?

BRICK. (*Crosses* d. l., *faces front.*) Yes, sir, yes, I know.

BIG DADDY. Is that why you quit sports-announcin', because of this liquor problem?

BRICK. Yes, sir, yes, sir, I guess so.

BIG DADDY. Son, don't guess about it, it's too important.

BRICK. (*Looks* r. *over Big Daddy's shoulder, into space.*) Yes, sir.

BIG DADDY. (*Crosses to Brick.*) An' listen to me—don't look at that dam' chandelier! (*Pause.*) Somethin' else we picked up at the big fire sale in Europe. Life is important. There's nothin' else to hold onto. A man that drinks is throwin' his life away. Don't do it. (*Brick crosses* r. *toward couch.*) Hold onto your life, there's nothin' else to hold onto. Son ——

BRICK. (*Sitting on* l. *end couch.*) Huh? (*Big Daddy coughs.*)

BIG DADDY. Whew! That cigar made me a little light-headed ——
(*Puts cigar in tray on bar.*) So you quit. How'd that come about? Some disappointment?

BRICK. I don't know, do you?

BIG DADDY. (*A step* r.) I'm askin' you. How in hell would I know if you don't? (*OFF* l., *A CLOCK CHIMES ELEVEN TIMES.*) [*Sound Cue 12.*] Why is it so damned hard for people to talk?

BRICK. That ole clock makes some nice remarks about time. I like to hear it all night.

BIG DADDY. (*Picks up Brick's crutch from the wicker seat against which Brick has placed it, and turns* c.) We got that clock the summer we went to Europe, me an' Big Mama on that damn' Cook's Tour, never had such a lousy time in my life! I'm tellin' you, son, those gooks over there, they gouge your eyeballs out in their grand hotels. An' Big Mama bought more stuff than you

41

could haul in a couple of box cars, that's no crap. Everywhere she went on this whirlwind tour she bought, bought, bought. Why, half that stuff she bought is still crated up an' mildewin' in the basement. Under water last spring! That Europe is nothin' on earth but a great big auction, that's all it is, that bunch of old, worn-out places, it's just a big fire sale, the whole ruttin' thing, an' Big Mama went wild in it! Why, you couldn't hold that woman with a mule's harness! Bought, bought, bought! Lucky I'm a rich man, yessiree, bob, it's lucky I'm a rich man, it sure is lucky, well, I am a rich man, Brick, yep, I'm a mighty rich man. (*Crosses to Brick.*) You know how much I'm worth? Guess, Brick. Guess how much I'm worth! Close on ten million in cash an' blue chip stocks outside, mind you, of 28,000 acres of the richest land this side of the Valley Nile! But a man can't buy his life with it, he can't buy back his life when his life has been spent, that's one thing not offered in th' Europe fire sale or in th' American markets or any markets on earth, a man can't buy his life with it, he can't buy back his life with it when his life is finished. . . . That's a sobering thought, a very sobering thought, and that's a thought that I was turning over in my head, over an' over an' over, until today—I'm wiser an' sadder, Brick, for this experience which I just gone through. They's one thing else I remember in Europe.
BRICK. What's that, Big Daddy?
BIG DADDY. (*Facing front,* D. S., *with crutch. Leaning on it.*) The hills around Barcelona in the country of Spain an' th' children runnin' over those bare hills in their bare skins, beggin' like starvin' dogs with howls an' screeches, an' how fat the priests are on th' streets of Barcelona, so many of 'em, an' so fat an' so pleasant. Y' know, I could feed that country? I got money enough to feed that goddam country, but the human animal is a selfish beast an' I don't reckon the money I passed out there to those howlin' children in th' hills around Barcelona would more than upholster one of the chairs in this room —— (*Crosses* R. C., *strikes seat with crutch. Turns front again.*) I mean pay to put a new cover on this chair! Well, I threw them money like you'd scatter feed corn for chickens, I threw money at 'em just to get rid of 'em long enough to climb back into th' car an' drive away. An' then in Morocco, them Arabs, why, prostitution begins at four or five, that's no exaggeration, why, I remember one day in Marrakesh, that old walled Arab city, I set on a broken-down wall to have a cigar, it

42

was fearful hot there an' this Arab woman stood in the road an' looked at me till I was embarrassed, she stood stock still in th' dusty hot road an' looked at me till I was embarrassed. But listen to this. She had a naked child with her, a little naked girl with her, barely able to toddle, an' after a while, she set this child on th' ground, whispered somethin' to her, an' give her a shove. This child come toward me, barely able t' walk, come toddlin' up to me an'—Jesus! It makes y' sick t' remember a thing like this! It stuck out its hand and tried to unbutton my trousers! That child was not yet five! Can you believe me? Or do you think that I am makin' this up? (*Turns* U. L. *with wide gesture with the crutch.*) I went back to the hotel an' said to Big Mama, "Big Mama! Git packed!" (*Big Mama appears for a moment on the* D. R. *gallery, listening, then goes out* D. R.) "We're clearin' out of this country!"

BRICK. Big Daddy, you're on a talkin' jag tonight.

BIG DADDY. Yes, sir, that's how it is, the human animal is a beast that dies but the fact that he's dyin' don't give him pity for others, no, sir, it —— (*Tosses Brick's crutch onto the bed.*)

BRICK. (*Softly.*) Gimme my crutch.

BIG DADDY. Did you say somethin'?

BRICK. Yes, sir.

BIG DADDY. What?

BRICK. Hand me over that crutch so I can get up.

BIG DADDY. Where you goin'?

BRICK. I'm takin' a little short trip to Echo Spring.

BIG DADDY. (*Gets crutch, crosses to Brick.*) Echo Spring? (*Hands Brick the crutch.*)

BRICK. (*Rising.*) Liquor cabinet. (*Starts* L. *for bar.*)

BIG DADDY. (*Intercepting Brick.*) Yes, sir, boy, the human animal is a beast that dies an' if he's got money he buys an' buys an' buys an' I think the reason he buys everything he can buy is that in the back of his mind he has the crazy hope that one of his purchases will be life everlastin'!—which it never can be—hear me?

BRICK. (*Moves above Big Daddy to bar.*) Big Daddy, you sure are shootin' the breeze here tonight.

BIG DADDY. (D. S. C.) I been quiet here lately, spoke not a word, just sat an' stared into space. I had somethin' heavy weighin' on my mind, but tonight that load was took off me. That's why I'm talkin'. The sky looks diff'rent to me!

BRICK. (*Holding bottle poised above his glass, at bar.*) You know what I like to hear most?

BIG DADDY. What?

BRICK. Solid quiet —— (*Pours.*) Perfect—(*Pours.*) unbroken— (*Pours.*) quiet. (*Pours.*)

BIG DADDY. Why?

BRICK. Because it's more peaceful.

BIG DADDY. Man, you'll be hearin' a lot of that soon enough in th' grave.

BRICK. Are you through talkin' to me?

BIG DADDY. (*Crosses* U. S. *to foot of bed, looking at Brick.*) Why are you so anxious to shut me up?

BRICK. (*Turns to Big Daddy.*) Well, sir, ever' so often you say to me, Brick, I want to have a talk with you, but when we talk, it never materializes. You gas about this an' that an' I look like I listen. I try to look like I listen, but I don't listen, not much. Big Daddy, communication between two people is very difficult, and somehow, between you an' me, it just does not happen.

BIG DADDY. (*Closer to Brick.*) Have you ever been scared? I mean have you ever felt downright terror of somethin'? (*Looks into hall, returns to* R. *of Brick.*) Son, I thought I had it. I thought the old man made out of bones had laid his cold an' heavy hand on my shoulder!

BRICK. Well, Big Daddy, you kept a tight mouth about it.

BIG DADDY. A pig squeals. A man keeps a tight mouth about it, in spite of a man not havin' a pig's advantage.

BRICK. What advantage is that?

BIG DADDY. Ignorance of mortality is a comfort. A man don't have that comfort, he's the only living thing that conceives of death, that knows what it is, the others go without knowing. A pig squeals, but a man, sometimes he can keep a tight mouth about it. I wonder if ——

BRICK. What, Big Daddy?

BIG DADDY. A whiskey highball would injure this spastic condition?

BRICK. (*Turning to bar.*) No, sir, it might do it good. (*Fixes drink for Big Daddy.*)

BIG DADDY. (*A step* D. R., *facing front.*) I can't tell you, boy! The sky is open! It's open again! It's open, boy, it's open!

BRICK. You feel better, Big Daddy?

BIG DADDY. Better? Hell! I can breathe! All my life I been like a doubled up fist—poundin', smashin', drivin'! Now I'm goin' to loosen these doubled up hands an' touch things *easy* with 'em. (*Brick crosses to Big Daddy at* c. *with drink. Taking the glass.*) You know what I'm contemplatin'?

BRICK. No, sir, what are you contemplatin'?

BIG DADDY. Pleasure! Pleasure with *women*. Yes, boy, I'll tell you something that you might not guess. I still have desire for women and this is my 65th birthday! (*Drinks.*)

BRICK. I think that's mighty remarkable, Big Daddy.

BIG DADDY. Remarkable?

BRICK. (*Crosses below Big Daddy to couch.*) *Admirable*, Big Daddy.

BIG DADDY. (*A step* R., *following Brick.*) You're goddam right it is, remarkable an' admirable both. I realize now that I never had me enough. I let many chances slip by because of scruples about it, scruples, convention, crap! All that stuff is bull! It took the shadow of death to make me see it. Now that shadow's lifted, I'm goin' to cut loose an' have, what is it they call it, have me a *ball!* (*PHONE, OFF* L.)

BRICK. A ball, huh? (*PHONE, OFF* L.)

BIG DADDY. That's right, a ball, a ball! (*PHONE, OFF* L.) Hell, I slept with Big Mama till, let's see, five years ago, till I was sixty an' she was fifty-eight, an' never even liked her, never did! (*Big Mama hurries in across lower gallery, from* R., *and rushes into the* D. S. *to door to the* L. *of Big Daddy who is standing beside Brick near the couch.*)

BIG MAMA. Don't you men hear that phone ring? I heard it way out on th' gall'ry. (*She pats kisses on Big Daddy's mouth, gaily.*)

BIG DADDY. There's five rooms off this front gall'ry that you could go through. Why do you go through this one? (*Big Mama laughs and exits into hall. Big Daddy steps upstage after her, looks into hall.*) When Big Mama goes out of a room, I can't remember what she looks like ——

BIG MAMA. (*Off* L., *on phone.*) Hello ——

BIG DADDY. But when Big Mama comes back into a room, boy, then I see what she looks like, an' I wish I didn't! (*Turns back to hall door, stands at* R. *end of bar.*)

BIG MAMA. (*Off, on phone.*) Hello, Miss Sally! (*Brick hobbles onto lower gallery.*)

45

BIG DADDY. Hey! Where you goin'?

BRICK. Out for a breather.

BIG DADDY. Not yet you ain't. Stay here till this talk is finished, young fellow.

BRICK. I thought it was finished, Big Daddy. (*OFF* L., *CLOCK CHIMES ONCE*.) *[Sound Cue 13.]*

BIG DADDY. It ain't even begun!

BRICK. I just wanted to feel that river breeze.

BIG MAMA. (*Off, on phone.*) Miss Sally, you're a caution, Miss Sally!

BIG DADDY. (*To Brick.*) Come back in here!

BRICK. My mistake, excuse me. (*Re-enters room.*)

BIG MAMA. (*Off, on phone.*) You didn't give me a chance to explain! (*Brick sits on* L. *end of couch, then lies back.*)

BIG DADDY. Jesus, she's talkin' to my old maid sister again.

BIG MAMA. (*Off, on phone.*) Now, you come down real soon, Miss Sally. Big Daddy's dyin' to see you!

BIG DADDY. (*Roaring.*) Bull! (*Puts his drink on the bar.*)

BIG MAMA. (*Off, on phone.*) Yaiss, good-bye, Miss Sally. (*Big Mama appears in hall, stands above Big Daddy, who has his back to door.*)

BIG MAMA. Big Daddy, that was Miss Sally callin'. She called her doctor in Memphis to git him to tell her what that spastic thing is! An' called back to tell me how relieved she was that —— Hey! Let me in!

BIG DADDY. Naw, I ain't. I tol' you not to come an' go through this room. You just back out an' go through those other five rooms.

BIG MAMA. (*Sneaking her arms around Big Daddy's waist.*) Big Daddy, Big Daddy, oh, Big Daddy! You didn't mean those things you said to me, did you? (*Big Mama gives Big Daddy a playful hug. It is sufficiently strong, however, to cause him to wince with pain. Unmindful, Big Mama scurries across the upper gallery, and pops into the* D. R. *doors, mincing toward the bed to pick up the birthday present, still lying there. Singing.*) Sweetheart, sweetheart! (*Gathering up the gift.*) Big Daddy, you didn't mean those awful things you said to me? I know you didn't. I know you didn't mean those things in your heart. (*Big Daddy roars at Big Mama. She trills lightly, and carries the gift out the* U. R. *doors, and exits on gallery,* R.)

BIG DADDY. (*Crosses* D. C., *facing front.*) All that I ask of that

woman is that she leave me alone. But she can't admit to herself
that she makes me sick. That comes of having slept with her too
many years. Should have quit much sooner, but that ole woman,
she never got enough of it. An' I was good in bed. I never should
have wasted so much of it on her. They say you got just so many
an' each one is numbered. Well, I got a few left in me, a few, an'
I'm goin' to pick me a good one to spend 'em on. I'm goin' to pick
me a choice one. I don't care how much she costs. I'll smother her
in minks! I'll strip her naked an' smother her in minks an' choke
her with diamonds! I'll strip her naked an' choke her with dia-
monds an' smother her with minks an' run her from Jackson to
Memphis—*non-stop!* (*Turns to Brick.*) Yes, son, I'm *happy.* I'm
happy, son, I'm happy! (*Brick rises, crosses below Big Daddy,
toward him.*) What makes you so restless? Have you got ants in
your britches?
BRICK. Yes, sir.
BIG DADDY. Why?
BRICK. Something—hasn't—happened.
BIG DADDY. Yeah, what is that?
BRICK. The—click.
BIG DADDY. (*Holds* D. S. R. C.) Did you say "click"?
BRICK. Yes, click.
BIG DADDY. What click?
BRICK. A click that I get in my head that makes me peaceful.
BIG DADDY. I sure in hell don't know what you're talkin'
about, but it disturbs me.
BRICK. (*Holding* D. L. C., *en route to bar, facing front.*) It's just
a mechanical thing. (*Drinks.*)
BIG DADDY. What is a mechanical thing?
BRICK. This click that I get in my head that makes me peaceful.
I got to drink till I get it. It's just a mechanical thing, something
like a—like a—like a —— (*Drinks.*)
BIG DADDY. Like a—what?
BRICK. (*Touching glass to forehead.*) Like a switch clicking off
in my head, turnin' the hot light off an' the cool light on, an' all of
a sudden there's peace!
BIG DADDY. Jesus! I didn't know it had gotten that bad with
you. Why, boy, you're *alcoholic!*
BRICK. That's the truth, Big Daddy. I'm alcoholic.
BIG DADDY. (*Speaks front.*) This shows how I let things go!

47

BRICK. I have to hear that little click in my head that makes me peaceful. (*Crosses to bar.*) Usually I hear it sooner than this, sometimes as early as noon, but today it's dilatory —— (*Pours drink.*) I just haven't got the right level of alcohol in my bloodstream yet. (*Drinks.*)

BIG DADDY. Expectin' death made me blind. I didn't have no idea that a son of mine was turnin' into a drunkard under my nose.

BRICK. Well, now you do, Big Daddy, the news has penetrated.

BIG DADDY. Yes, now I do. The news has—penetrated.

BRICK. And so if you'll excuse me ——

BIG DADDY. (*Turns to Brick.*) No, I won't excuse you.

BRICK. (*Below bar, facing front.*) I'd better sit by myself till I hear that click in my head, it's just a mechanical thing but it don't happen except when I'm alone or talkin' to no one.

BIG DADDY. (*Crosses to R. of Brick.*) You got a long, long time to sit still, boy, and talk to no one, but now you're talkin' to me. At least I'm talkin' to you. An' you set there an' listen until I tell you the conversation is over!

BRICK. (*Turns to Big Daddy.*) But this talk is like all the others we've ever had together in our lives! It's nowhere, nowhere! It's— it's *painful*, Big Daddy!

BIG DADDY. All right, then, let it be painful! (*Big Daddy pulls Brick's crutch out from beneath his arm. The crutch falls. Big Daddy pushes Brick to the wicker seat, D. R. C., and forces him to sit. Brick clings to his drink.*)

BRICK. I can hop on one foot, an' if I fall, I can crawl!

BIG DADDY. If you ain't careful you're goin' to crawl off this plantation an' then, by Jesus, you'll have to hustle your drinks along Skid Row!

BRICK. That'll come, Big Daddy.

BIG DADDY. No, it won't! You're my son an' I'm goin' to straighten you out, now that *I'm* straightened out, I'm goin' to straighten you out!

BRICK. Yeah? (*Starts to rise.*)

BIG DADDY. (*Pushes him back.*) Stay here, you son of a bitch, till I say go!

BRICK. I can't. (*Tries to rise.*)

BIG DADDY. (*Pushes him back.*) You sure in hell will, God damn it!

BRICK. No, I can't. We talk, you talk—in circles! We get nowhere. You say you want to talk to me and don't have a thing to say to me. (*Big Mama appears on gallery,* R., *listening.*)

BIG DADDY. Nothin' to say when I tell you I'm goin' to live when I thought I was dyin'!

BRICK. Oh—*that!* Is that what you have to say to me?

BIG DADDY. Why, you son of a bitch! Ain't that, ain't that—*important?*

BRICK. Well, you said that, that's said, and now I —— (*Starts to rise.*)

BIG DADDY. (*Pushes him back.*) Now you set back down!

BRICK. You're all balled up!

BIG DADDY. I ain't balled up!

BRICK. You are, you're all balled up! (*Starts up.*)

BIG DADDY. (*Pushing him back.*) Don't tell me what I am, you drunken whelp!

BRICK. Big Daddy ——

BIG DADDY. I want you to know I'm back in the driver's seat now!

BIG MAMA. (*At* U. R. *doors, apprehensively.*) Big Daddy—why ——?

BIG DADDY. (*Crosses above wicker seat to Big Mama.*) What in hell do you want here, Big Mama? (*Brick, released, scrambles for his crutch. He leaves his drink on the couch.*)

BIG MAMA. Oh, Big Daddy! Why are you shoutin' like that? I just cain't stainnnd it! I tell you, I just cain't ——

BIG DADDY. *GIT OUTA HERE!* (*Brick secures his crutch* C., *starts to hobble toward* D. S. *gallery door. Big Daddy turns, crosses to him, seizes the crutch from under Brick's arm, catapulting Brick face-down onto the catwalk of the* D. S. *gallery. Big Mama cries out, and starts along lower gallery at* R. *toward Brick.*) Leave him alone! (*Miserably, with a backward look, Big Mama goes out at* R. *on gallery.*)

BRICK. Christ ——!

BIG DADDY. (*Standing in* D. S. *doorway.*) Yeah! Christ!—is right.

BRICK. Big Daddy—give me my crutch! Give me my crutch, Big Daddy.

BIG DADDY. Why do you drink?

BRICK. Don't know—give me my crutch!

BIG DADDY. You better think why you drink or give up drinkin'!

BRICK. Will you please give me my crutch so I can get up off this floor?

BIG DADDY. First you answer my question. Why do you drink? Why are you throwin' your life away, boy, like somethin' disgustin' you picked up on the street?

BRICK. (*Struggling toward drink on end of the couch.*) Big Daddy, I'm in pain, I stepped on that foot.

BIG DADDY. (*Knocking the glass to the floor. u. s.*) Good! I'm glad you're not too numb with liquor in you to feel some pain!

BRICK. You—spilled my drink.

BIG DADDY. I'll make a bargain with you. You tell me why you drink an' I'll hand you one. I'll pour you the liquor myself an' hand it to you.

BRICK. Why do I drink?

BIG DADDY. Yeah—why?

BRICK. Give me a drink and I'll tell you.

BIG DADDY. Tell me first!

BRICK. I'll tell you in one word.

BIG DADDY. What word?

BRICK. DISGUST! (*OFF L., CLOCK CHIMES TWICE. [Sound Cue 14.] Brick struggles to his feet.*) Now how about that drink?

BIG DADDY. What are you disgusted with? You got to tell me that, first. Otherwise bein' disgusted don't make no sense.

BRICK. Give me my crutch ——

BIG DADDY. You heard me, you got to tell me what I asked you first.

BRICK. I told you, I said to kill my disgust!

BIG DADDY. DISGUST WITH WHAT?! (*Exhausted, Brick stumbles across the step into Big Daddy's arms.*)

BRICK. You strike a hard bargain.

BIG DADDY. (*Holding Brick, speaks almost gently.*) You want liquor that bad?

BRICK. (*Clinging to Big Daddy.*) Yeah, I want it that bad.

BIG DADDY. (*Pats Brick, consolingly.*) If I give you a drink will you tell me what it is you're disgusted with, Brick?

BRICK. Yes, sir, I will try to. (*Big Daddy helps Brick to sit on L. end of couch. He pats his head, gently. DISTANTLY, THREE HAWK CRIES. [Sound Cue 15.] Big Daddy gets Brick's crutch, hands it to Brick, stands beside the boy.*) Have you ever heard the word "mendacity"?

BIG DADDY. Sure. Mendacity is one of them five dollar words that cheap politicians throw back an' forth at each other.

BRICK. You know what it means?

BIG DADDY. Don't it mean lyin' an' liars?

BRICK. Yes, sir, lyin' an' liars.

BIG DADDY. Has someone been lyin' to you? (*Gooper hurries onto* R. *gallery. In the lawn area, marching on from* U. R., *Mae shepherds the monsters in a parade. Sonny leads, beating a drum, his arm firmly held by Mae. Then comes Buster, followed by Dixie and Trixie, who wave sparklers.*)

MAE AND CHILDREN. (*Chanting, with Gooper's encouragement.*)

We want Big Dad-dee!

We want Big Dad-dee!

(*The procession pauses* U. S. C. *above hall doorway, in lawn area, and the chant continues. Gooper hurries into the room from hall door. Big Daddy shouts "Jesus!" crosses to Gooper,* U. C.)

GOOPER. Big Daddy, the kiddies are shoutin' for you out there.

BIG DADDY. Keep out, Gooper!

GOOPER. 'Scuse me! (*Gooper goes out through hall door, pantomimes to Mae to take the children out* U. L. *in lawn area. They go, without another sound. Gooper drifts out,* R. *along gallery. Big Daddy crosses to bar to pour Brick's drink.*)

BIG DADDY. Who's been lyin' to you? Has Margaret been lyin' to you, has your wife been lyin' to you about somethin', Brick?

BRICK. Not her. That wouldn't matter.

BIG DADDY. Then who's been lyin' to you, an' what about?

BRICK. No one single person an' no one lie.

BIG DADDY. Then what, what then? Then who, about what?

BRICK. (*Rubs head.*) The whole, the whole—thing.

BIG DADDY. (*Crosses to Brick with drink.*) Why are you rubbin' your head? You got a headache?

BRICK. No, I'm tryin' to ——

BIG DADDY. (*Hands Brick the drink.*) Concentrate, but you can't because your brain's all soaked with liquor, is that the trouble? Wet brain! What do you know about this mendacity thing? Hell, I could write a book on it! (*Crosses* D. C., *faces front.*) I could write a book on it an' still not cover the subject! Well, I could, I could write a goddam book on it an' still not cover th' subject anywhere near enough! Think of all th' lies I got to put up with! Pre-

51

tenses! Ain't that mendacity? Havin' to pretend stuff you don't think or feel or have any idea of? Havin' for instance to act like I care for Big Mama! I haven't been able to stand the sight, sound or smell of that woman for forty years! Church! It bores the bejesus out of me, but I go! I go an' sit there an' listen to that dam' fool preacher! Clubs! Elks! Masons! Rotary! (*Turns to Brick.*) *You* I *do* like for some reason, did always have some kind of real feelin' for—affection—respect —— (*Bows on each word.*) Yes, always, I don't know why, but it is! (*Crosses to Brick.*) *I've* lived with mendacity! Why can't *you* live with it? Hell, you *got* to live with it, there's nothin' *else* to *live* with except mendacity, is there?

BRICK. Yes, sir, yes, sir, there is somethin' else that you can live with.

BIG DADDY. What?

BRICK. (*Raising glass.*) This!

BIG DADDY. That's not livin', that's dodgin' away from life.

BRICK. (*Drinks.*) I want to dodge away from it.

BIG DADDY. Then why don't you kill yourself, man?

BRICK. I like to drink.

BIG DADDY. God! I can't talk to you. (*Crosses* U. C.)

BRICK. I'm sorry, Big Daddy.

BIG DADDY. (*Turns to Brick from* C.) Not as sorry as I am. I'll tell you somethin'. A little while back when I thought my number was up, before I found out it was just this—spastic—colon, I thought about you. Should I or should I not, if the jig was up, give you this place when I go? I hate Gooper an' those five screamin' monkeys like parrots in a jungle an' that bitch Mae! Why should I turn over 28,000 acres of the richest land this side of the Valley Nile to not my kind? But why in hell on the other hand, Brick, should I subsidize a dam' fool on the bottle? Liked or not liked, well, maybe even—loved! Why should I do that? Subsidize worthless behavior? Rot? Corruption? (*Crosses* D. C., *face front.*) An' this I will tell you frankly. I didn't make up my mind at all on that question an' still to this day I ain't made out no will! Well, now I don't *have* to! The pressure is gone. (*Crosses to Brick.*) I can just wait an' see if you pull yourself together or if you don't.

BRICK. That's right, Big Daddy.

BIG DADDY. You sound like you thought I was kiddin'.

BRICK. (*Rises.*) No, sir, I know you're not kiddin'.

BIG DADDY. But you don't care ——?

BRICK. (*Crosses above couch to* R. *gallery doors.*) No, sir, I don't care ——

BIG DADDY. WAIT! WAIT, BRICK. (*Crosses to above wicker seat, facing Brick.*) Don't let's leave it like this, like them other talks we've had, we've always—talked around things, we've—just talked around things like some rotten reason, I don't know what, it's always like somethin' was left not spoken, somethin' avoided because neither of us was honest enough with the other ——

BRICK. I never lied to you, Big Daddy.

BIG DADDY. Did I ever to *you*?

BRICK. No, sir.

BIG DADDY. (*His arm on Brick's arm.*) Then there is at least two people that never lied to each other.

BRICK. Yes, sir, but we've never *talked* to each other.

BIG DADDY. We can *now*.

BRICK. Big Daddy, there don't seem to be anything much to say.

BIG DADDY. You say that you drink to kill your disgust with lyin'.

BRICK. You said to give you a reason.

BIG DADDY. Is liquor the only thing that'll kill this disgust?

BRICK. Now. Yes.

BIG DADDY. But not once, huh?

BRICK. Not when I was still young an' believin'. A drinkin' man's someone who wants to forget he isn't still young an' believin'.

BIG DADDY. Believin' what?

BRICK. (*Starts back for* D. S. *gallery door.*) Believin' ——

BIG DADDY. (*Following, above wicker seat, to* L. *of Brick at door,* D. S.) Believin' what?

BRICK. Believin' . . .

BIG DADDY. I don't know what th' hell you mean by believin', an' I don't think you know what you mean by believin', but if you still got sports in your blood, go back to sports announcin' an' ——

BRICK. Sit in a glass box watchin' games I can't play. Describin' what I can't do while players do it? Sweatin' out their disgust an' confusion in contests I'm not fit for? Drinkin' a coke, half bourbon, so I can stand it? That's no dam' good any more—time just outran me, Big Daddy—got there first.

53

BIG DADDY. (*Turns to Brick.*) I think you're passin' the buck.

BRICK. You know many drinkin' men?

BIG DADDY. I have known a fair number of that species.

BRICK. Could any of 'em tell you why they drank?

BIG DADDY. (*Crosses to Brick.*) Yep, you're passin' the buck, you're passin' the buck to things like time an' disgust with mendacity, an'—crap! If you got to use that kind of language about a thing it's 90-proof bull an' I'm not buyin' any.

BRICK. I had to give you a reason to get a drink.

BIG DADDY. What did you say?

BRICK. I said: I had to give you a reason to get a drink.

BIG DADDY. You started drinkin' when your friend Skipper died! (*Pause.*)

BRICK. What are you suggestin'?

BIG DADDY. I'm suggestin' nothin'—(*Brick starts for the bar, crossing below Big Daddy.*) but Gooper an' Mae suggested that there was somethin' not right, exactly, in your ——

BRICK. "Not right" ——?

BIG DADDY. (*Starts C.*) Not, well, exactly *normal* in your—friendship with ——

BRICK. (*Turning back to Big Daddy, L. C.*) They suggested that, too? I thought that was Maggie's suggestion. Who else's suggestion is it, is it *yours?* How many others thought that Skipper and I were ——?

BIG DADDY. Now hold on, hold on a minute, son. I knocked around in my time ——

BRICK. What's that got to do with it? (*Rev. Tooker enters from R. on gallery and eases into the room through doors R. to behind wicker seat.*)

BIG DADDY. (*Crosses D. C., front.*) I said "Hold on"! I bummed, I bummed this country till ——

BRICK. (*Following.*) Whose suggestion—who else's suggestion is it?

BIG DADDY. Slept in hobo jungles an' railroad Y's an' flop-houses in all cities before ——

BRICK. Oh, *you* think so, too, you call me your son and a queer! (*Rev. Tooker clears his throat. Big Daddy swings around to face Rev. Tooker above wicker seat. Brick turns D. C.*)

BIG DADDY. Preacher! What're you lookin' for, Preacher?

REV. TOOKER. The gentlemen's lavatory ——

54

BIG DADDY. Go back out an' walk down to th' other end of th' gall'ry, Rev'rend, an' use th' bathroom connected with my bed-room, an' if you can't find it, ask 'em where it is! (*Bows Rev. Tooker out R. gallery.*)

REV. TOOKER. Ah—thanks —— (*Goes L. on gallery through hall and out. OFF L., CLOCK CHIMES THREE TIMES.*) [*Sound Cue 16.*]

BIG DADDY. (*Crosses to above Brick, at his R.*) Look, Brick, I can understand, I can understand anything. Christ! The year I came here, in 1910, I wore my shoes through, hocked my gear, hopped off a yellow dog freight car half a mile down th' road, slep in a wagon of cotton outside th' gin—Jack Straw an' Peter Ochello took me in, hired me to manage this place, which grew into this one—when Jack Straw died, why, ole Peter Ochello quit eatin' like a dog does when it's master's dead, an' died, too!

BRICK. Christ!

BIG DADDY. I'm just sayin' I understand such ——

BRICK. Skipper is dead—I have not quit eatin'!

BIG DADDY. No, but you started drinkin'.

BRICK. (*Whirls on him.*) YOU THINK SO, TOO! (*Circles above Big Daddy to his R.*) You think so, too? You think me an' Skipper did, did, did—sodomy—together?

BIG DADDY. (*Turning to Brick.*) Hold ——

BRICK. That what you ——?

BIG DADDY. —ON—a minute!

BRICK. You think we did dirty things between us, Skipper an' ——

BIG DADDY. Who are you shoutin' like that? Why are you ——

BRICK. —me, is that what you think of Skipper, is that ——

BIG DADDY. —so excited? I don't think nothin'. I don't know nothin'. I'm simply telling you what ——

BRICK. You think Skipper an' me were a pair of dirty ole men?

BIG DADDY. Now, that's ——

BRICK. Straw? Ochello? A couple of ——

BIG DADDY. Now just ——

BRICK. —duckin' sissies? Queers? Is that what ——? (*Strikes out at Big Daddy.*)

BIG DADDY. Take it easy, son.

BRICK. —think? (*Brick loses his balance, stumbles against Big Daddy, his face averted.*)

BIG DADDY. Jesus! Whew! Grab my hand!

55

BRICK. (*Turns, starts for bed.*) Naw—I don't want your hand! (*Falls head down across* L. *side of bed.*)

BIG DADDY. (*Crosses below Brick to below bed, leans over, touching Brick's shoulder.*) Well, I want yours. Git up. You broken out in a sweat!! You're pantin' like you run a mile— (*Sits at Brick's* R. *on foot of bed.*)

BRICK. (*Gradually raising himself.*) Big Daddy, you shock me, Big Daddy, you, you—*shock* me! Talkin' so—casually—about a thing—like that. Don't you know how people *feel* about things like that? How, how *disgusted* they are by things like that? Why, at Ole Miss, when it was discovered that a pledge in our fraternity, Skipper's an' mine, did a, *attempted* to do a—unnatural thing with —— We not only dropped him like a hot rock, we told him to git off the campus, an' he did, he got!—all the way to ——

BIG DADDY. Where?

BRICK. North Africa, last I heard!

BIG DADDY. Well, I have come back from further away than that, I just now returned from the other side of the moon, death's country, son, an' I'm not easy to shock by anything here. Always, anyhow, lived with too much space around me to be infected by th' ideas of other people. One thing you can grow on a big place more important than cotton—is *tolerance!* I grown it.

BRICK. (*Sitting up, recovering crutch.*) Why can't exceptional friendship, *real, real, deep, deep friendship* between two men be respected as somethin' clean an' decent without bein' thought of as—*fairies!*

BIG DADDY. It can, it is, for God's sake. I told Mae an' Gooper ——

BRICK. To hell with Mae an' Gooper! (*Rises, crosses* D. S.) To hell with all dirty lies an' liars! Skipper an' me had a clean, true thing between us, had a clean friendship practically all our lives, till Maggie got the idea you're talkin' about. Normal? No. It was too rare to be normal, any true thing between two people is too rare to be normal. Oh, once in a while he put his hand on my shoulder or I'd put mine on his, oh, maybe even when we were tourin' the country in pro football an' sharin' hotel rooms, we'd reach across the space between th' two beds an' shake hands to say good night, yeah, one or two times we ——

BIG DADDY. (*Circling above Brick to* C.) Brick, nobody thinks that's not normal!

56

BRICK. Well, they're mistaken! It was! It was a pure an' true thing an' that's not normal! (*Across the horizon, a burst of fireworks. [Sound Cue 17.] Mae and children appear in the lawn area,* U. R.)

MAE. Big Daddy, they're startin' the fireworks! (*Mae and children run off,* U. R. *Shouts, whistles and applause accompany the burst of fireworks, which dies out.*)

BIG DADDY. (*A step to* L. C.) Yeah—it's hard t'—talk.

BRICK. All right, then—let's let it go.

BIG DADDY. No, sir! Why did Skipper crack up? Why have you?

BRICK. (*Crosses above to* L. C., *toward bar.*) All right. You're askin' for it, Big Daddy. We're finally goin' to have that real, true talk you wanted. It's too late to stop it now, we got to carry it through an' cover ev'ry subject. (*Fireworks reflected* U. R. *Cheers, whistles, etc., off* U. R. *Brick turns to bar, picks up bottle, puts it down, turns to Big Daddy.*) Maggie declares that Skipper an' I went into pro football after we left Ole Miss because we were scared to grow up, wanted to keep on tossin' those long, long, high, high passes that couldn't be intercepted except by time, th' aerial attack that made us famous! An' so we did, we did, we kept it up for one season, that aerial attack, we held it high! Yeah, but—that summer Maggie, she laid down the law to me—(*Crosses* D. L. C. *to front.*) said now or never, and so I married Maggie.

BIG DADDY. (R. C., *facing front.*) How was Maggie in bed?

BRICK. Great! She went on the road that Fall with th' Dixie Stars. Oh, she made a great show of bein' the world's best sport. She wore a tall bearskin cap! (*Fireworks reflected* U. R. *Cheers, whistles, etc., off* U. R.) A shake, they call it, a dyed moleskin coat, a moleskin coat dyed red. Cut up crazy! Rented hotel ball rooms for victory celebrations, wouldn't cancel 'em when it turned out—defeat. MAGGIE TH' CAT! But Skipper, he had some fever which came back on him which the doctors couldn't explain, an' I got that injury—turned out to be just a shadow on th' X-ray plate, an' a touch of bursitis. I lay in a hospital bed, watched out games on TV, saw Maggie on the bench next to Skipper when he was hauled out of the game for stumbles, fumbles!—burned me up the way she hung on his arm! Y' know I think that Maggie had always felt sort of left out, so she took this time to work on poor dumb Skipper! Poured in his mind the dirty, false idea that what we

57

were, him an' me was a frustrated case of that ole pair of sisters that lived in this room, Jack Straw an' Peter Ochello! He, poor Skipper, went to bed with Maggie to prove it wasn't true, an' when it didn't work out, he thought it *was* true! Skipper broke in two like a rotten stick—nobody ever turned so fast into a lush— or died of it so quick. Now—are you satisfied?

BIG DADDY. Are you satisfied?

BRICK. With what?

BIG DADDY. That story.

BRICK. What's wrong with it? (*OFF* L. *PHONE RINGS.*)

BIG DADDY. Not completed. Something's left out —— (*OFF* L. *PHONE RINGS.*) What did you leave out?

GOOPER. (*Answering phone, off* L.) Hello ——

BRICK. Yes, I left out a long distance phone call which I had from Skipper ——

GOOPER. (*Off* L.) Speaking. Go ahead ——

BRICK. —in which he made a drunken confession to me an' on which I hung up.

GOOPER. (*Off* L.) No.

BRICK. Last time we spoke to each other in our lives.

GOOPER. (*Off* L.) No, sir.

BIG DADDY. (*Crosses toward Brick.*) You musta said *somethin'* to him before you hung up.

BRICK. What could I say to him?

BIG DADDY. *Anything!—something!*

BRICK. Nothing.

BIG DADDY. You just hung up?

BRICK. Just hung up.

BIG DADDY. Uh-huh. (*Brick turns* U. S., *Big Daddy crosses to above Brick, then to Brick's* R., *as Brick turns* D. S.) Anyhow now we have tracked down the lie with which you're disgusted an' which you are drinkin' to kill your disgust with. It wasn't Maggie. Maggie, nothin'! It was you! You been passin' the buck. This disgust with mendacity is disgust with yourself! You dug the grave of your friend an' kicked him in it!—before you'd face truth with him!

BRICK. (*Turns to Big Daddy.*) *His* truth, not *mine!*

BIG DADDY. His truth, okay, but you wouldn't face it with him!

BRICK. Who *can* face truth? Can *you?*

BIG DADDY. Now don't start passin' th' rotten buck again, boy!

58

BRICK. *How about these birthday congratulations, these many, many happy returns of th' day, when ev'rybody but you knows there won't be any!* (*Pause.*) Let's—let's go out now, let's go out now, let's go out now an' watch the fireworks. (*Slaps himself, starts through* C. *to* R.) Come on, Big Daddy ——

BIG DADDY. Oh, no! No one's goin' out! What did you start to say?

BRICK. (*At* R. *gallery good.*) I don't remember ——

BIG DADDY. Many happy returns ——

BRICK. Aw, hell, Big Daddy ——

BIG DADDY. When there won't be any ——?

BRICK. Forget it. Come on out on the gall'ry an' look at th' fireworks they're shootin' off for your birthday.

BIG DADDY. First, you finish that remark you were makin'.

BRICK. Look, now, Big Daddy ——

BIG DADDY. FINISH! FINISH WHAT YOU WAS SAYIN'!

BRICK. Leave th' place to Gooper an' Mae an' their five little same monkeys. All I want is ——

BIG DADDY. LEAVE TH' PLACE—did you say?

BRICK. All 28,000 acres of th' richest land this side of th' Valley Nile.

BIG DADDY. Who said I was leavin' the place to Gooper or anybody? This is my sixty-fifth birthday. I got fifteen, twenty years left in me! I'll outlive *you!* I'll bury you! I'll buy your coffin!

BRICK. Sure. Many happy returns. Now let's go watch the fireworks, come on, let's ——

BIG DADDY. Brick, have they been lyin'? About the report from th' clinic? Did they—did they find—somethin'? *Cancer*—maybe?

BRICK. Mendacity is a system that we live in. (*Off* R. *the field hands commence singing. Song continues until curtain. Mae and Gooper hurry into lawn area,* U. R.)

MAE. Oh, Big Daddy, th' field hands are singin' fo' you!

GOOPER. Field hands singin' fo' you, sir. (*Mae and Gooper hurry out,* U. R. *Big Daddy stands transfixed,* D. L. C. *Brick hobbles to him.*)

BRICK. I'm sorry, Big Daddy. My head don't work any more. Maybe it's bein' alive that makes people lie, an' bein' almost not alive makes me sort of accidentally truthful. I don't know, but anyway, we've been friends—an' being friends is tellin' each other th'

59

truth. You told me! I told you! (*Drops his head against Big Daddy's shoulder.*)

BIG DADDY. (*Shouting, suddenly.*) CHRIST—DAMN——

GOOPER. (*Off* U. R., *managing the fireworks display.*) Let—'er —go——! (*Off* U. R. *and across the horizon,* THE FIREWORKS BLAZE FURIOUSLY.) [*Sound Cue 18.*]

BIG DADDY. (*Crossing* U. S. C., *out hall door, and along* R. *gallery.*) —DAMN ALL—LYIN' SONS OF—LYIN' BITCHES! YES—ALL LIARS, ALL LIARS, ALL LYIN', DYIN' LIARS! LYIN'—DYIN'—LIARS! LIARS! LIARS! (*THE LIGHTS DIM OUT.*)

CURTAIN

ACT III

Big Daddy is seen leaving as at the end of Act II.

BIG DADDY. (*Shouts, as he goes out* D. R. *on gallery.*) ALL—
LYIN'—DYIN'—LIARS! LIARS! LIARS! (*After Big Daddy has
gone, Margaret enters from* D. R. *on gallery, into room through*
D. S. *door. She crosses to Brick at* L. C.)
MARGARET. Brick, what in the name of God was goin' on in
this room? (*Dixie and Trixie rush through the room from the hall,*
L. *to gallery* R. *brandishing cap pistols, which they fire repeatedly,
as they shout: "Bang! Bang! Bang!" Mae appears from* D. R. *gal-
lery entrance, and turns the children back* U. L., *along gallery. At
the same moment, Gooper, Rev. Tooker and Dr. Baugh enter from*
L. *in the hall.*)
MAE. Dixie! You quit that! Gooper, will y' please git these kiddies
t' baid? Right now? (*Gooper and Rev. Tooker cross along upper
gallery. Dr. Baugh holds,* U. C., *near hall door. Rev. Tooker crosses
to Mae near section of gallery just outside doors,* R.)
GOOPER. (*Urging the children along.*) Mae—you seen Big
Mama?
MAE. Not yet. (*Dixie and Trixie vanish through hall,* L.)
REV. TOOKER. (*To Mae.*) Those kiddies are so full of vitality.
I think I'll have to be startin' back to town. (*Margaret turns to
watch and listen.*)
MAE. Not yet, Preacher. You know we regard you as a member
of this fam'ly, one of our closest an' dearest, so you just got t' be
with us when Doc Baugh gives Big Mama th' actual truth about th'
report from th' clinic. (*Calls through door.*) Has Big Daddy gone
to bed, Brick? (*Gooper has gone out* D. R. *at the beginning of the
exchange between Mae and Rev. Tooker.*)
MARGARET. (*Replying to Mae.*) Yes, he's gone to bed. (*To
Brick.*) Why'd Big Daddy shout "liars"?
GOOPER. (*Off* D. R.) Mae! (*Mae exits* D. R. *Rev. Tooker drifts
along upper gallery.*)

BRICK. I didn't lie to Big Daddy. I've lied to nobody, nobody but myself, just lied to myself. The time has come to put me in Silver Hill, put me in Silver Hill, Maggie, I ought to go there.
MARGARET. Over my dead body! (*Brick starts* R. *She holds him.*) Where do you think you're goin'? (*Mae enters from* D. R. *on gallery, crosses to Rev. Tooker, who comes to meet her.*)
BRICK. (*Crosses below to* C.) Out for some air, I want air ——
GOOPER. (*Entering from* D. R. *to Mae, on gallery.*) Now, where is that old lady?
MAE. Can'tcha find her, Gooper? (*Rev. Tooker goes out* D. R.)
GOOPER. (*Crosses to* D. C. *above hall door.*) She's avoidin' this talk.
MAE. I think she senses somethin'.
GOOPER. (*Calls off* L.) Sookey! Go find Big Mama an' tell her Doc Baugh an' the Preacher've got to go soon.
MAE. Don't let Big Daddy hear yuh! (*Brings Dr. Baugh to* R. *on gallery.*)
REV. TOOKER. (*Off* D. R., *calls.*) Big Mama!
SOOKEY AND DAISY. (*Running from* L. *to* R. *in lawn. Calling.*) Miss Ida! Miss Ida! (*They go out* U. R.)
GOOPER. (*Calling off upper gallery.*) Lacey, you look downstairs for Big Mama!
MARGARET. Brick, they're going to tell Big Mama the truth now, an' she needs you! (*Rev. Tooker appears in lawn area,* U. R., *crosses* C.)
DR. BAUGH. (*To Mae, on* R. *gallery.*) This is going to be painful.
MAE. Painful things can't always be avoided.
DR. BAUGH. That's what I've noticed about 'em, Sister Woman.
REV. TOOKER. (*On lawn, points off* R.) I see Big Mama! (*Hurries off* L. *and re-appears shortly in hall.*)
GOOPER. (*Hurrying into hall.*) She's gone round the gall'ry to Big Daddy's room. Hey, Mama! (*Off.*) Hey, Big Mama! Come here!
MAE. (*Calls.*) Hush, Gooper! Don't holler, go to her! (*Gooper and Rev. Tooker now appear together in hall. Big Mama runs in from* D. R., *carrying a glass of milk. She crosses past Dr. Baugh to Mae, on* R. *gallery. Dr. Baugh turns away.*)
BIG MAMA. Here I am! What d' you all want with me?
GOOPER. (*Steps toward Big Mama.*) Big Mama, I told you we got to have this talk.

BIG MAMA. What talk you talkin' about? I saw the light go on in Big Daddy's bedroom an' took him his glass of milk, an' he just shut the shutters right in my face. (*Steps into room through* R. *door.*) When old couples have been together as long as me an' Big Daddy they, they get irritable with each other just from too much—devotion! Isn't that so? (*Crosses below wicker seat to* R. C. *area.*)

MARGARET. (*Crosses to Big Mama, embracing her.*) Yes, of course it's so. (*Brick starts out* U. C. *through hall, but sees Gooper and Rev. Tooker entering, so he hobbles through* C. *out* D. S. *door and onto gallery.*)

BIG MAMA. I think Big Daddy was just worn out. He loves his fam'ly. He loves to have 'em around him, but it's a strain on his nerves. He wasn't himself tonight, Brick —— (*Crosses toward Brick. Brick passes her on his way out,* D. S.) Big Daddy wasn't himself, I could tell he was all worked up.

REV. TOOKER. (U. S. C.) I think he's remarkable.

BIG MAMA. Yaiss! Just remarkable. (*Faces* U. S., *turns, crosses to bar, puts down glass of milk.*) Did you notice all the food he ate at that table? (*Crosses* R. *a bit.*) Why, he ate like a hawss!

GOOPER. (U. S. C.) I hope he don't regret it.

BIG MAMA. (*Turns* U. S. *toward Gooper.*) What! Why, that man ate a huge piece of cawn bread with molasses on it! Helped himself twice to hoppin' john!

MARGARET. (*Crosses to Big Mama.*) Big Daddy loves hoppin' john. We had a real country dinner.

BIG MAMA. Yais, he simply adores it! An' candied yams. Son —— (*Crosses to* D. S. *door, looking out at Brick. Margaret crosses above Big Mama to her* L.) That man put away enough food at that table to stuff a field hand.

GOOPER. I hope he don't have to pay for it later on.

BIG MAMA. (*Turns* U. S.) What's that, Gooper?

MAE. Gooper says he hopes Big Daddy doesn't suffer tonight.

BIG MAMA. (*Turns to Margaret,* D. C.) Oh, shoot, Gooper says, Gooper says! Why should Big Daddy suffer for satisfyin' a nawmal appetite? There's nothin' wrong with that man but nerves, he's sound as a dollar! An' now he knows he is, an' that's why he ate such a supper. He had a big load off his mind, knowin' he wasn't doomed to—what—he thought he was—doomed t' —— (*She wavers. Margaret puts her arms around Big Mama.*)

63

GOOPER. (*Urging Mae forward.*) MAE! (*Mae runs forward below wicker seat. She stands below Big Mama, Margaret above Big Mama. They help her to the wicker seat. Big Mama sits. Margaret sits above her. Mae stands behind her.*)

MARGARET. Bless his ole sweet soul.

BIG MAMA. Yes—bless his heart.

BRICK. (D. S. *on gallery, looking out front.*) Hello, moon, I envy you, you cool son of a bitch.

BIG MAMA. I want Brick!

MARGARET. He just stepped out for some fresh air.

BIG MAMA. Honey! I want Brick!

MAE. Bring li'l Brother in here so we kin talk. (*Margaret rises, crosses through* D. S. *door to Brick on gallery.*)

BRICK. (*To the moon.*) I envy you—you cool son of a bitch.

MARGARET. Brick, what're you doin' out here on the gall'ry, baby?

BRICK. Admirin' an' complimentin' th' man in the moon. (*Mae crosses to Dr. Baugh on* R. *gallery. Rev. Tooker and Gooper move* R. U. C., *looking at Big Mama.*)

MARGARET. (*To Brick.*) Come in, baby. They're gettin' ready to tell Big Mama the truth.

BRICK. I can't witness that thing in there.

MAE. Doc Baugh, d' you think those vitamin B12 injections are all they're cracked up t' be? (*Enters room to upper side, behind wicker seat.*)

DR. BAUGH. (*Crosses to below wicker seat.*) Well, I guess they're as good t' be stuck with as anything else. (*Looks at watch. Crosses through to* L. C.)

MARGARET. (*To Brick.*) Big Mama needs you!

BRICK. I can't witness that thing in there!

BIG MAMA. What's wrong here? You all have such long faces, you sit here waitin' for somethin' like a bomb—to go off.

GOOPER. We're waitin' for Brick an' Maggie to come in for this talk.

MARGARET. (*Crosses above Brick, to his* R.) Brother Man an' Mae have got a trick up their sleeves, an' if you don't go in there t' help Big Mama,

BIG MAMA. Talk. Whispers! Whispers! (*Looks out* D. R.) Brick! . . . Never had this sort of atmosphere here before.

64

y' know what I'm goin' to
do ——? (*Answers Big Mama's
call.*) Comin', Big Mama! (*To
Brick.*) I'm goin' to take every
dam' bottle on this place an'
pitch it off th' levee into th'
river!

MAE. (*Sits above Big Mama on wicker seat.*) Before what, Big
Mama?
BIG MAMA. This occasion. What's Brick an' Maggie doin' out
there now?
GOOPER. (*Crosses* D. C., *looks out.*) They seem to be havin'
some little altercation. (*Brick crosses toward* D. S. *step. Maggie
moves* R. *above him to portal* D. R. *Rev. Tooker joins Dr. Baugh,*
L. C.)
BIG MAMA. (*Taking a pill from pill box on chain at her wrist.*)
Give me a little somethin' to wash this tablet down with. Smell of
burnt fireworks always makes me sick. (*Mae crosses to bar to pour
glass of water. Dr. Baugh joins her. Gooper crosses to Rev. Tooker,*
L. C.)
BRICK. (*To Margaret.*) You're a live cat, aren't you?
MARGARET. You're dam' right I am!
BIG MAMA. Gooper, will y' please open that hall door—an' let
some air circulate in this stiflin' room? (*Gooper starts* U. S., *but is
restrained by Mae who crosses through* C. *with glass of water.
Gooper turns to men* D. L. C.)
MAE. (*Crosses to Big Mama with water, sits above her.*) Big
Mama, I think we ought to keep that door closed till after we talk.
BIG MAMA. I swan! (*Drinks water. Washes down pill.*)
MAE. I just don't think we ought to take any chance of Big Daddy
hearin' a word of this discussion.
BIG MAMA. (*Hands glass to Mae.*) What discussion of what?
Maggie! Brick! Nothin' is goin' to be said in th' house of Big
Daddy Pollitt that he can't hear if he wants to! (*Mae rises, crosses
to bar, puts down glass, joins Gooper and the two men,* L. C.)
BRICK. How long are you goin' to stand behind me, Maggie?
MARGARET. Forever, if necessary. (*Brick crosses* U. S. *to* R.
gallery door.)
BIG MAMA. Brick! (*Mae rises, looks out* D. S., *sits.*)

65

GOOPER. That boy's gone t' pieces—he's just gone t' pieces.

DR. BAUGH. Y' know, in my day they used to have somethin' they called the Keeley Cure for drinkers.

BIG MAMA. Shoot!

DR. BAUGH. But nowadays, I understand they take some kind of tablets that kill their taste for the stuff.

GOOPER. (*Turns to Dr. Baugh.*) Call 'em anti-bust tablets.

BIG MAMA. Brick don't need to take nothin'. That boy is just broken up over Skipper's death. You know how poor Skipper died. They gave him a big, big dose of that sodium amytal stuff at his home, an' then they called the ambulance an' give him another big, big dose of it at th' hospital an' that an' all the alcohol in his system fo' months an' months just proved too much for his heart an' his heart quit beatin'. I'm scared of needles! I'm more scared of a needle than th' knife —— (*Brick has entered the room to behind the wicker seat. He rests his hand on Big Mama's head. Gooper has moved a bit U. R. C., facing Big Mama.*) Oh! Here's Brick! My precious baby! (*Dr. Baugh crosses to bar, puts down drink. Brick crosses below Big Mama through C. to bar.*)

BRICK. Take it, Gooper!

MAE. (*Rising.*) What?

BRICK. Gooper knows what. Take it, Gooper! (*Mae turns to Gooper U. R. C. Dr. Baugh crosses to Rev. Tooker. Margaret, who has followed Brick U. S. on R. gallery before he entered the room, now enters room, to behind wicker seat.*)

BIG MAMA. (*To Brick.*) You just break my heart.

BRICK. (*At bar.*) Sorry—anyone else?

MARGARET. Brick, sit with Big Mama an' hold her hand while we talk.

BRICK. You do that, Maggie. I'm a restless cripple. I got to stay on my crutch. (*Mae sits above Big Mama. Gooper moves in front, below, and sits on couch, facing Big Mama. Rev. Tooker closes in to R. C. Dr. Baugh crosses D. C., faces upstage, smoking cigar. Margaret turns away to R. doors.*)

BIG MAMA. Why're you all *surroundin'* me?—like this? Why're you all starin' at me like this an' makin' signs at each other? (*Brick hobbles out hall door and crosses along R. gallery.*) I don't need nobody to hold my hand. Are you all crazy? Since when did Big Daddy or me need anybody ——? (*Rev. Tooker moves behind wicker seat.*)

66

MAE. Calm yourself, Big Mama.

BIG MAMA. Calm you'self *you'self*, Sister Woman! How could I calm myself with everyone starin' at me as if big drops of blood had broken out on m' face? What's this all about, Annh! What?

GOOPER. Doc Baugh —— (*Mae rises.*) Sit down, Mae —— (*Mae sits.*) Big Mama wants to know the complete truth about th' report we got today from the Ochsner Clinic! (*Dr. Baugh buttons his coat, faces group at* R. C.)

BIG MAMA. Is there somethin'—somethin' that I don't know?

DR. BAUGH. Yes—well . . .

BIG MAMA. (*Rises.*) I—want to—*knowwwww!* (*Crosses to Dr. Baugh.*) Somebody must be lyin'! *I want to know!* (*Mae, Gooper, Rev. Tooker surround Big Mama.*)

MAE. Sit down, Big Mama, sit down on this sofa! (*Brick has passed Margaret crossing* D. R. *on gallery.*)

MARGARET. Brick! Brick!

BIG MAMA. *What is it, what is it?* (*Big Mama drives Dr. Baugh a bit* D. L. C. *Others follow, surrounding Big Mama.*)

DR. BAUGH. I never have seen a more thorough examination than Big Daddy Pollitt was given in all my experience at the Ochsner Clinic.

GOOPER. It's one of th' best in th' country.

MAE. It's *THE* best in th' country—bar none!

DR. BAUGH. Of course they were ninety-nine and nine-tenths percent certain before they even started.

BIG MAMA. Sure of what, sure of what, sure of what—*what!?*

MAE. Now, Mommy, be a brave girl!

BRICK. (*On* D. R. *gallery, covers his ears, sings.*) "By the light, by the light of the silvery moon!"

GOOPER. (*Break* D. R., *calls out to Brick.*) Shut up, Brick! (*Returns to group* L. C.)

BRICK. Sorry. . . . (*Continues singing.*)

DR. BAUGH. But now, you see, Big Mama, they cut a piece off this growth, a specimen of the tissue, an' ——

BIG MAMA. Growth? You told Big Daddy ——

DR. BAUGH. Now, wait ——

BIG MAMA. You told me an' Big Daddy there wasn't a thing wrong with him but ——

MAE. Big Mama, they always ——

GOOPER. Let Doc Baugh talk, will yuh?

67

BIG MAMA. —little spastic condition of ——

REV. TOOKER. (*Throughout all this.*) *Shh! Shh! Shh!* (*Big Mama breaks* U. C., *they all follow.*)

DR. BAUGH. Yes, that's what we told Big Daddy. But we had this bit of tissue run through the laboratory an' I'm sorry t' say the test was positive on it. It's malignant. (*Pause.*)

BIG MAMA. *Cancer! Cancer!*

MAE. Now, now, Mommy ——

GOOPER. (*At the same time.*) You had to know, Big Mama.

BIG MAMA. *Why didn't they cut it out of him? Hanh? Hannh?*

DR. BAUGH. Involved too much, Big Mama, too many organs affected.

MAE. Big Mama, the liver's affected, an' so's the kidneys, both. It's gone way past what they call a ——

GOOPER. —a surgical risk. (*Big Mama gasps.*)

REV. TOOKER. Tch, tch, tch.

DR. BAUGH. Yes, it's gone past the knife.

MAE. That's why he's turned yellow! (*Brick stops singing, turns away* U. R. *on gallery.*)

BIG MAMA. (*Pushes Mae* D. S.) Git away from me, git away from me, Mae! (*Crosses* D. S. R.) I want Brick! Where's Brick! *Where's my only son?*

MAE. (*A step after Big Mama.*) Mama! Did she say "only" son?

GOOPER. (*Following Big Mama.*) What does that make me?

MAE. (*Above Gooper.*) A sober responsible man with five precious children—*six!*

BIG MAMA. I want Brick! Brick! Brick!

MARGARET. (*A step to Big Mama above couch.*) Mama, let *me* tell you.

BIG MAMA. (*Pushing her aside.*) No, no, leave me alone, you're not my blood! (*She rushes onto the* D. S. *gallery.*)

GOOPER. (*Crosses to Big Mama on gallery.*) Mama! I'm your son! Listen to me!

MAE. Gooper's your son, Mama, he's your first born!

BIG MAMA. Gooper never liked Daddy!

MAE. That's not true!

REV. TOOKER. (U. C.) I think I'd better slip away at this point. Good night, good night, everybody, and God bless you all—on this place. (*Goes out through hall.*)

DR. BAUGH. (*Crosses* D. R. *to above* D. S. *door.*) Well, Big Mama ——

BIG MAMA. (*Leaning against Gooper, on lower gallery.*) It's all a mistake, I know it's just a bad dream.

DR. BAUGH. We're gonna keep Big Daddy as comfortable as we can.

BIG MAMA. Yes, it's just a bad dream, that's all it is, it's just an awful dream.

GOOPER. In my opinion Big Daddy is havin' some pain but won't admit that he has it.

BIG MAMA. Just a dream, a bad dream.

DR. BAUGH. That's what lots of 'em do, they think if they don't admit they're havin' the pain they can sort of escape th' fact of it. (*Brick crosses* U. S. *on* R. *gallery. Margaret watches him from* R. *doors.*)

GOOPER. Yes, they get sly about it, get real sly about it.

MAE. (*Crosses to* R. *of Dr. Baugh.*) Gooper an' I think ——

GOOPER. Shut up, Mae!—Big Mama, I really do think Big Daddy should be started on morphine.

BIG MAMA. (*Pulling away from Gooper.*) Nobody's goin' t' give Big Daddy morphine!

DR. BAUGH. Now, Big Mama, when that pain strikes it's goin' to strike mighty hard an' Big Daddy's goin' t' need the needle to bear it.

BIG MAMA. (*Crosses to Dr. Baugh.*) I tell you, nobody's goin' to give him morphine!

MAE. Big Mama, you don't want to see Big Daddy suffer, y' know y' ——

DR. BAUGH. (*Crosses to bar.*) Well, I'm leavin' this stuff here (*Puts packet of morphine, etc., on bar.*) so if there's a sudden attack you won't have to send out for it. (*Big Mama hurries to* L. *side bar.*)

MAE. (*Crosses* C., *below Dr. Baugh.*) I know how to give a hypo.

BIG MAMA. Nobody's goin' to give Big Daddy morphine!

GOOPER. (*Crosses* C.) Mae took a course in nursin' durin' the war.

MARGARET. Somehow I don't think Big Daddy would want Mae t' give him a hypo.

MAE. (*To Margaret.*) You think he'd want *you* to do it?

DR. BAUGH. Well ——

69

GOOPER. Well, Dr. Baugh is goin' ——
DR. BAUGH. Yes, I got to be goin'. Well, keep your chin up, Big Mama. (*Crosses to ball.*)
GOOPER. (*As he and Mae follow Dr. Baugh into the hall.*) She's goin' to keep her ole chin up, aren't you, Big Mama? (*They go out* L.) Well, Doc, we sure do appreciate all you've done. I'm telling you, we're obligated ——
BIG MAMA. Margaret! (*Crosses* R. C.)
MARGARET. (*Meeting Big Mama in front of wicker seat.*) I'm right here, Big Mama.
BIG MAMA. Margaret, you've got to cooperate with me an' Big Daddy to straighten Brick out now ——
GOOPER. (*Off* L., *returning with Mae.*) I guess that doctor has got a lot on his mind, but it wouldn't hurt him to act a little more human ——
BIG MAMA. —because it'll break Big Daddy's heart if Brick don't pull himself together an' take hold of things here. (*Brick crosses* D. S. R. *on gallery.*)
MAE. (U. C., *overhearing.*) Take hold of what things, Big Mama?
BIG MAMA. (*Sits in wicker chair, Margaret standing behind chair.*) The place.
GOOPER. (U. C.) Big Mama, you've had a shock.
MAE. (*Crosses with Gooper to Big Mama.*) Yais, we've all had a shock, but ——
GOOPER. Let's be realistic ——
MAE. Big Daddy would not, would *never*, be foolish enough to ——
GOOPER. —put this place in irresponsible hands!
BIG MAMA. Big Daddy ain't goin' t' put th' place in anybody's hands, Big Daddy is *not* goin' t' die! I want you to git that into your haids, all of you! (*Mae sits above Big Mama. Margaret turns* R. *to door. Gooper crosses* L. C. *a bit.*)
MAE. Mommy, Mommy, Big Mama, we're just as hopeful an' optimistic as you are about Big Daddy's prospects, we have faith in prayer—but nevertheless there are certain matters that have to be discussed an' dealt with because otherwise ——
GOOPER. Mae, will y' please get my brief case out of our room?
MAE. Yes, honey. (*Rises, goes out through hall* L.)
MARGARET. (*Crosses to Brick on* D. S. *gallery.*) Hear them in there? (*Crosses back to* R. *gallery door.*)

GOOPER. (*Stands above Big Mama. Leaning over her.*) Big
Mama, what you said just now was not at all true, an' you know it.
I've always loved Big Daddy in my own quiet way. I never made
a show of it. I know that Big Daddy has always been fond of me
in a quiet way, too. (*Margaret drifts* U. R. *on gallery. Mae returns,
crosses to Gooper's* L. *with briefcase.*)
MAE. Here's your briefcase, Gooper, honey. (*Hands it to him.*)
GOOPER. (*Hands briefcase back to Mae.*) Thank you. Of cou'se
my relationship with Big Daddy is different from Brick's.
MAE. You're eight years older'n Brick an' always had t' carry a
bigger load of th' responsibilities than Brick ever had t' carry, he
never carried a thing in his life but a football or a highball.
GOOPER. Mae, will y' let me talk, please?
MAE. Yes, honey.
GOOPER. Now, a 28,000 acre plantation's a mighty big thing t'
run.
MAE. Almost single-handed!
BIG MAMA. You never had t' run this place, Brother Man, what're
you talkin' about, as if Big Daddy was dead an' in his grave, you
had to run it? Why, you just had t' help him out with a few business details an' had your law practice at the same time in Memphis.
MAE. Oh, Mommy, Mommy, Mommy! Let's be fair! Why,
Gooper had given himself body an' soul t' keepin' this place up
fo' the past five years since Big Daddy's health started failin'.
Gooper won't say it, Gooper never thought of it as a duty, he just
did it. An' what did Brick do? Brick kep' livin' in his past glory
at college! (*Gooper places a restraining hand on Mae's leg. Margaret drifts* D. S. *in gallery.*)
GOOPER. Still a football player at 27!
MARGARET. (*Bursts into* U. R. *door.*) Who are you talkin' about
now? Brick? A football player? He isn't a football player an' you
know it! Brick is a sports announcer on TV an' one of the best
known ones in the country!
MAE. (*Breaks* U. C.) I'm talkin' about what he was!
MARGARET. (*Crosses to above lower gallery door.*) Well, I wish
you would just stop talkin' about my husband!
GOOPER. (*Crosses to above Margaret.*) Listen, Margaret, I've
got a right to discuss my own brother, with other members of my
own fam'ly, which don't include you! (*Pokes finger at her, she*

slaps his finger away.) Now, why don't you go on out there an' drink with Brick?

MARGARET. I've never seen such malice toward a brother.

GOOPER. How about his for me? Why, he can't stand to be in the same room with me!

BRICK. (*On lower gallery.*) That's the truth!

MARGARET. This is a deliberate campaign of vilification for the most disgusting and sordid reason on earth, and I know what it is! *It's avarice, avarice, greed, greed!*

BIG MAMA. Oh, I'll scream, I will scream in a moment unless this stops! Margaret, child, come here, sit next to Big Mama.

MARGARET. (*Crosses to Big Mama, sits above her.*) Precious Mommy. (*Gooper crosses to bar.*)

MAE. How beautiful, how touchin' this display of devotion! Do you know why she's childless? She's childless because that big, beautiful athlete husband of hers won't go to bed with her, that's why! (*Crosses to L. of bed, looks at Gooper.*)

GOOPER. You jest won't let me do this the nice way, will yuh? Aw right —— (*Crosses to above wicker seat.*) I don't give a goddam if Big Daddy likes me or don't like me or did or never did or will or will never! I'm just appealin' to a sense of common decency an' fair play! I'm tellin' you th' truth —— (*Crosses D. S. through lower door to Brick on D. R. gallery.*) I've resented Big Daddy's partiality to Brick ever since th' goddam day you were born, son, an' th' way I've been treated, like I was just barely good enough to spit on, an' sometimes not even good enough for that. (*Crosses back through room to above wicker seat.*) Big Daddy is dyin' of cancer an' it's spread all through him an' it's attacked all his vital organs includin' the kidneys an' right now he is sinkin' into uremia, an' you all know what uremia is, it's poisonin' of the whole system due to th' failure of th' body to eliminate its poisons.

MARGARET. Poisons, poisons, venomous thoughts and words! In hearts and minds! That's poisons!

GOOPER. I'm askin' for a square deal an' by God, I expect to get one. But if I don't get one, if there's any peculiar shenanigans goin' on around here behind my back, well, I'm not a corporation lawyer for nothin'! (*Crosses D. S. toward lower gallery door, on apex.*) I know how to protect my own interests. (*RUMBLE OF DISTANT THUNDER.*) [*Sound Cue 19.*]

72

BRICK. (*Entering the room through* D. S. *door.*) Storm comin' up.

GOOPER. Oh, a late arrival!

MAE. (*Crosses through* C. *to below bar*, L. C.) Behold, the conquerin' hero comes!

GOOPER. (*Crosses through* C. *to bar, following Brick, imitating his limp.*) The fabulous Brick Pollitt! Remember him? Who could forget him?

MAE. He looks like he's been injured in a game!

GOOPER. Yep, I'm afraid you'll have to warm th' bench at the Sugar Bowl this year, Brick! Or was it the Rose Bowl that he made his famous run in. (*ANOTHER RUMBLE OF THUNDER. SOUND OF WIND RISING.*) [*Sound Cue 20.*]

MAE. (*Crosses to* L. *of Brick, who has reached the bar.*) The punch bowl, honey, it was the punch bowl, the cut-glass punch bowl!

GOOPER. That's right! I'm always gettin' the boy's *bowls* mixed up! (*Pats Brick on the butt.*)

MARGARET. (*Rushes at Gooper, striking him.*) Stop that! You stop that! (*Thunder offstage. Mae crosses toward Margaret from* L. *of Gooper, flails at Margaret, Gooper keeps the women apart. Lacey runs through the* U. S. *lawn area in a raincoat.*)

DAISY AND SOOKEY. (*Off* U. L.) Storm! Storm comin'! Storm! Storm!

LACEY. (*Running out* U. R.) Brightie, close them shutters!

GOOPER. (*Crosses onto* R. *gallery, calls after Lacey.*) Lacey, put the top up on my Cadillac, will yuh?

LACEY. (*Off* R.) Yes, suh, Mistah Pollitt!

GOOPER. (*Crosses to above Big Mama.*) Big Mama, you know it's goin' to be necessary for me t' go back to Memphis in th' mornin' t' represent the Parker estate in a lawsuit. (*Mae sits on* L. *side bed, arranges papers she removes from brief case.*)

BIG MAMA. Is it, Gooper?

MAE. Yaiss.

GOOPER. That's why I'm forced to—to bring up a problem that ——

MAE. Somethin' that's too important t' be put off!

GOOPER. If Brick was sober, he ought to be in on this. I think he ought to be present when I present this plan.

MARGARET. (U. C.) Brick is present, we're present!

73

GOOPER. Well, good. I will now give you this outline my partner Tom Bullit an' me have drawn up—a sort of dummy-trusteeship!

MARGARET. Oh, that's it. You'll be in charge an' dole out remittances, will you?

GOOPER. This we did as soon as we got the report on Big Daddy from th' Ochsner Laboratories. We did this thing, I mean we drew up this dummy outline with the advice and assistance of the Chairman of the Boa'd of Directors of th' Southern Plantuhs Bank & Trust Company in Memphis, C. C. Bellowes, a man who handles estates for all th' prominent fam'lies in West Tennessee and th' Delta!

BIG MAMA. Gooper?

GOOPER. (*Crosses behind seat to below Big Mama.*) Now this is not—not final, or anything like it, this is just a preliminary outline. But it does provide a—basis—a design—a—possible, feasible —plan! (*He waves papers Mae has thrust into his hand, u. s.*)

MARGARET. (*Crosses D. L.*) Yes, I'll bet it's a plan! (*THUNDER ROLLS. INTERIOR LIGHTING DIMS.*) [*Sound Cue 21.*]

MAE. It's a plan to protect the biggest estate in the Delta from irresponsibility an' ——

BIG MAMA. Now you listen to me, all of you, you listen here! They's not goin' to be no more catty talk in my house! And, Gooper, you put that away before I grab it out of your hand and tear it right up! I don't know what the hell's in it, and I don't want to know what the hell's in it: I'm talkin' in Big Daddy's language now, I'm his *wife*, not his *widow*, I'm still his *wife*! And I'm talkin' to you in his language an' ——

GOOPER. Big Mama, what I have here is ——

MAE. Gooper explained that it's just a plan . . .

BIG MAMA. I don't care what you got there, just put it back where it come from an' don't let me see it again, not even the outside of the envelope of it! Is that understood? Basis! Plan! Preliminary! Design!—I say—what is it that Big Daddy always says when he's disgusted? (*STORM CLOUDS RACE ACROSS SKY.*)

BRICK. (*From bar.*) Big Daddy says "crap" when he is disgusted.

BIG MAMA. (*Rising.*) That's right—CRAPPP! I say CRAP too, like Big Daddy! (*THUNDER ROLLS.*) [*Sound Cue 22.*]

MAE. Coarse language don't seem called for in this ——

GOOPER. Somethin' in me is *deeply outraged* by this. *Nobody's goin' to do nothin'!* till Big Daddy lets go of it, and maybe just

74

possibly not—not even then! No, not even then! *[Sound Cue 23.]* (*THUNDER CLAP. GLASS CRASH, OFF* L. *Off* U. R., *children commence crying. Many storm sounds,* L. *and* R.: *barnyard animals in terror, papers crackling, shutters rattling. Sookey and Daisy hurry from* L. *to* R. *in lawn area. Inexplicably, Daisy hits together two leather pillows. They cry, "Storm! Storm!" Sookey waves a piece of wrapping paper to cover lawn furniture. Mae exits to hall and upper gallery. Strange man runs across lawn,* R. *to* L. *THUNDER ROLLS REPEATEDLY.*) *[Sound Cue 23 ends.]*

MAE. Sookey, hurry up an' git that po'ch furniture covahed; want th' paint to come off? (*Starts* D. R. *on gallery. Gooper runs through hall to* R. *gallery.*)

GOOPER. (*Yells to Lacey, who appears from* R.) Lacey, put mah car away!

LACEY. Cain't, Mistah Pollitt, you got the keys! (*Exit* U. S.)

GOOPER. Naw, you got 'em, man. (*Exit* D. R. *Re-appears* U. R., *calls to Mae.*) Where th' keys to th' car, honey? (*Runs* C.)

MAE. (D. R. *on gallery.*) You got 'em in your pocket! (*Exits* D. R. *Gooper exits* U. R. *Dog howls. [Sound Cue 24.] Daisy and Sookey sing off* U. R. *to comfort children. Mae is heard placating the children. STORM FADES AWAY. During the storm, Margaret crosses and sits on couch,* D. R. *Big Mama crosses* D. C.)

BIG MAMA. BRICK! Come here, Brick, I need you. (*THUNDER DISTANTLY. [Sound Cue 25.] Children whimper off* L. *Mae consoles them. Brick crosses to* R. *of Big Mama.*) Tonight Brick looks like he used to look when he was a little boy just like he did when he played wild games in the orchard back of the house and used to come home when I hollered myself hoarse for him! all—sweaty—and pink-cheeked—an' sleepy with his curls shinin' ——— (*THUNDER DISTANTLY. [Sound Cue 26.] Children whimper, off* L. *Mae consoles them. Dog howls, off.*) Time goes by so fast. Nothin' can outrun it. Death commences too early—almost before you're half-acquainted with life—you meet with the other. Oh, you know we just got to love each other, an' stay together all of us just as close as we can, specially now that such a *black* thing has come and moved into this place without invitation. (*DOG HOWLS OFF.*) *[Sound Cue 27.]* Oh, Brick, son of Big Daddy, Big Daddy does so love you. Y' know what would be his fondest dream come true? If before he passed on, if Big Daddy has to pass on . . . (*DOG HOWLS OFF.*) *[Sound Cue 28.]* You give him a child of

75

yours, a grandson as much like his son as his son is like Big Daddy. . . .

MARGARET. I know that's Big Daddy's dream.

BIG MAMA. That's his dream.

BIG DADDY. (*Off* D. R. *on gallery.*) Looks like the wind was takin' liberties with this place. (*Lacey appears* U. L., *crosses to* U. C. *in lawn area, Brightie and Small appear* U. R. *on lawn. Big Daddy crosses onto the* U. R. *gallery.*)

LACEY. 'Evenin', Mr. Pollitt.

BRIGHTIE AND SMALL. 'Evenin', Cap'n. Hello, Cap'n.

MARGARET. (*Crosses to* R. *door.*) Big Daddy's on the gall'ry.

BIG DADDY. Stawm crossed th' river, Lacey?

LACEY. Gone to Arkansas, Cap'n. (*Big Mama has turned toward the hall door at the sound of Big Daddy's voice on the gallery. Now she crosses* D. S. R. *and out the* D. S. *door onto the gallery.*)

BIG MAMA. I can't stay here. He'll see somethin' in my eyes.

BIG DADDY. (*On upper gallery, to the boys.*) Stawm done any damage around here?

BRIGHTIE. Took the po'ch off ole Aunt Crawley's house.

BIG DADDY. Ole Aunt Crawley should of been settin' on it. It's time fo' th' wind to blow that ole girl away! (*Field hands laugh, exit,* U. R. *Big Daddy enters room,* U. C., *hall door. He is wearing a cashmere bathrobe and slippers.*) Can I come in? (*Puts his cigar in ash tray on bar. Mae and Gooper hurry along the upper gallery and stand behind Big Daddy in hall door.*)

MARGARET. Did the storm wake you up, Big Daddy?

BIG DADDY. Which stawm are you talkin' about—th' one outside or th' hullaballoo in here? (*Gooper squeezes past Big Daddy.*)

GOOPER. (*Crosses toward bed. And legal papers strewn on bed.*) 'Scuse me, sir. . . . (*Mae tries to squeeze past Big Daddy to join Gooper, but Big Daddy puts his arm firmly around her.*)

BIG DADDY. I heard some mighty loud talk. Sounded like somethin' important was bein' discussed. What was the pow-wow about?

MAE. (*Flustered.*) Why—nothin', Big Daddy. . . .

BIG DADDY. (*Crosses* D. L. C., *taking Mae with him.*) What is that pregnant-lookin' envelope you're puttin' back in your brief case, Gooper?

GOOPER. (*At foot of bed, caught, as he stuffs papers into envelope.*) That? Nothin', suh—nothin' much of anythin' at all. . . .

BIG DADDY. Nothin', huh? Looks like a whole lot of nuthin',

76

don't it? Well, I just got one more question to ask. (*Sniffs.*) What is the smell in this room? Don't you notice it, Brick? Don't you notice a powerful and obnoxious odor of mendacity in this room?

BRICK. Yes, sir, I think I do, sir.

GOOPER. Mae, Mae . . .

BIG DADDY. (*To Mae, whom he still holds beside him, at his R.*) There is nothing more powerful. (*Turns to Brick.*) Is there, Brick? (*Released, Mae hurries to Gooper.*)

BRICK. No, sir. No, sir, there isn't, an' nothin' more obnoxious.

BIG DADDY. Brick agrees with me —— (*Gooper and Mae whisper together, below bed. He hands her briefcase, she turns toward hall door, as if to go. Big Daddy wheels on them.*) The odor of mendacity is a powerful and obnoxious odor an' the stawm hasn't blown it away from this room yet. You notice it, Gooper?

GOOPER. What—sir?

BIG DADDY. How about you, Sister Woman? You notice the unpleasant odor of mendacity in this room?

MAE. (*Concealing briefcase behind her.*) Why, Big Daddy, I don't even know what that is. (*Gooper relieves Mae of the briefcase, stows it at D. R. corner of bed.*)

BIG DADDY. (*Crosses D. C., to point.*) You can smell it. Hell! It smells like Death! (*On the lower gallery, Big Mama sobs. Big Daddy looks toward her.*) What's wrong with that long, thin woman over there, loaded with diamonds? Hey, what's-your-name, what's the matter with you?

MARGARET. (*Crosses toward Big Daddy.*) She had a slight dizzy spell, Big Daddy.

BIG DADDY. (U. L. C.) You better watch that, Big Mama. A stroke is a bad way to go.

MARGARET. (*Crosses to Big Daddy at C.*) Oh, Brick, Big Daddy has on your birthday present to him. Brick, he has on your cashmere robe, the softest material I have ever felt.

BIG DADDY. Yeah, this is my soft birthday, Maggie. . . . (*SONG BEGINS, OFF R.*) Not my gold or my silver birthday, but my soft birthday, everything's got to be soft for Big Daddy on this soft birthday. (*Maggie kneels before Big Daddy C. As Gooper and Mae speak, Big Mama crosses U. S. R. C. in front of them, hushing them with a gesture.*)

GOOPER. Maggie, I hate to make such a crude observation, but there is somethin' a little indecent about your ——

77

MAE. Like a slow-motion football tackle ——

MARGARET. Big Daddy's got on his Chinese slippers that I gave him, Brick. Big Daddy, I haven't given you my big present yet, but now I will, now's the time for me to present it to you! I have an announcement to make!

MAE. What? What kind of announcement?

GOOPER. A sports announcement, Maggie?

MARGARET. Announcement of life beginning! A child is coming, sired by Brick, and out of Maggie the Cat! I have Brick's child in my body, an' that's my birthday present to Big Daddy on this birthday! (*Big Daddy looks at Brick who crosses behind Big Daddy to* D. S. *portal,* L.)

BIG DADDY. Get up, girl, get up off your knees, girl. (*Big Daddy helps Margaret rise. He crosses above her, to her* R., *bites off the end of a fresh cigar [taken from his bathrobe pocket], as he studies Margaret.*) *Uh-huh, this girl has life in her body, that's no lie!*

BIG MAMA. BIG DADDY'S DREAM COME TRUE!

BRICK. *JESUS!*

BIG DADDY. (*Crosses* R. *below wicker seat.*) Gooper, I want my lawyer in the mornin'.

BRICK. Where are you goin', Big Daddy?

BIG DADDY. Son, I'm goin' up on the roof to the belvedere on th' roof to look over my kingdom before I give up my kingdom— 28,000 acres of th' richest land this side of the Valley Nile! (*Exits through* R. *doors, and* D. R. *on gallery.*)

BIG MAMA. (*Following.*) Sweetheart, sweetheart, sweetheart— can I come with you? (*Exits* D. R. *Margaret is* D. S. C. *in mirror area.*)

GOOPER. (*Crosses to bar.*) Brick, could you possibly spare me one small shot of that liquor?

BRICK. (D. L. C.) Why, help yourself, Gooper boy.

GOOPER. I will.

MAE. (*Crosses forward.*) Of course we know that this is a lie!

GOOPER. (*Drinks.*) Be still, Mae!

MAE. (*Crosses to Gooper at bar.*) I won't be still! I know she's made this up!

GOOPER. God damn it, I said to shut up!

MAE. That woman isn't pregnant!

GOOPER. Who said she was?

MAE. She did!

GOOPER. The doctor didn't. Doc Baugh didn't.

MARGARET. (*Crosses* R. *to above couch.*) I haven't gone to Doc Baugh.

GOOPER. (*Crosses through to* L. *of Margaret.*) Then who'd you go to, Maggie? (*SONG FINISHES.*)

MARGARET. One of the best gynecologists in the South.

GOOPER. Uh-huh, I see —— (*Foot on end of couch, trapping Margaret.*) May we have his name please?

MARGARET. No, you may not, Mr.—Prosecutin' Attorney!

MAE. (*Crosses to* R. *of Margaret, above.*) He doesn't have any name, he doesn't exist!

MARGARET. He does so exist, and so does my baby, Brick's baby!

MAE. You can't conceive a child by a man that won't sleep with you unless you think you're —— (*Forces Margaret onto couch, turns away* C. *Brick starts* C. *for Mae.*) He drinks all the time to be able to tolerate you! Sleeps on the sofa to keep out of contact with you!

GOOPER. (*Crosses above Margaret, who lies face down on couch.*) Don't try to kid us, Margaret ——

MAE. (*Crosses to bed,* L. *side, rumpling pillows.*) How can you conceive a child by a man that won't sleep with you? How can you conceive? How can you? How can you!

GOOPER. (*Sharply.*) *MAE!*

BRICK. (*Crosses below Mae to her* R., *takes hold of her.*) Mae, Sister Woman, how d' you know that I don't sleep with Maggie?

MAE. We occupy the next room an' th' wall between isn't sound proof.

BRICK. Oh. . . .

MAE. We hear the nightly pleadin' and the nightly refusal. So don't imagine you're goin' t' put a trick over on us, to fool a dyin' man with—a ——

BRICK. Mae, Sister Woman, not everybody makes much noise about love. Oh, I know some people are huffers an' puffers, but others are silent lovers.

GOOPER. (*Behind seat,* R.)   BRICK. How d' y' know that
This talk is pointless, com-   we're not silent lovers?
pletely.

BRICK. Even if y' got a peep-hole drilled in the wall, how can

79

y' tell if sometimes when Gooper's got business in Memphis an'
you're playin' scrabble at the country club with other ex-queens
of cotton, Maggie and I don't come to some temporary agreement?
How do you know that ——? (*He crosses above wicker seat to
above* R. *end couch.*)
MAE. Brick, I never thought that you would stoop to her level, I
just never dreamed that you would stoop to her level.
GOOPER. I don't think Brick will stoop to her level.
BRICK. (*Sits* R. *of Margaret on couch.*) What is your level? Tell
me your level so I can sink or rise to it. (*Rises.*) You heard what
Big Daddy said. This girl has life in her body.
MAE. That is a lie!
BRICK. No, truth is something desperate, an' she's got it. Believe
me, it's somethin' desperate, an' she's got it. (*Crosses below seat
to below bar.*) An' now if you will stop actin' as if Brick Pollitt
was dead an' buried, invisible, not heard, an' go on back to your
peep-hole in the wall—I'm drunk, and sleepy—not as alive as
Maggie, but still alive. . . . (*Pours drink, drinks.*)
GOOPER. (*Picks up brief case from* R. *foot of bed.*) Come on,
Mae. We'll leave these love birds together in their nest.
MAE. Yeah, nest of lice! Liars!
GOOPER. Mae—Mae, you jes' go on back to our room ——
MAE. Liars! (*Exits through hall.*)
GOOPER. (D. R. *above Margaret.*) We're jest goin' to wait an'
see. Time will tell. (*Crosses to* R. *of bar.*) Yes, sir, little brother,
we're jest goin' to wait an' see! (*Exit, hall. THE CLOCK STRIKES
TWELVE. [Sound Cue 29.] Maggie and Brick exchange a look.
He drinks deeply, puts his glass on the bar. Gradually, his expression changes. He utters a sharp exhalation. The exhalation is
echoed by the singers, off* U. R., *who commence vocalizing with
"Gimme a Cool Drink of Water 'Fo' I Die.")*
MARGARET. (*As she hears Brick's exhalation.*) The click? (*Brick
looks toward the singers, happily, almost gratefully. He crosses to
bed, picks up his pillow and starts toward head of couch,* D. R.,
*crossing above wicker seat. Margaret seizes the pillow from his
grasp, rises, stands facing* C., *holding the pillow close. Brick watches
her with growing admiration. She moves quickly* U. S. C., *throwing
pillow onto bed. She crosses to bar. Brick counters below wicker
seat, watching her. Margaret grabs all the bottles from the bar.
She goes into hall, pitches the bottles, one after the other, off the*

platform into the u. l. *lawn area. Bottles break, off* l. *Margaret re-enters the room, stands* u. c., *facing Brick.*) Echo Spring has gone dry, and no one but me could drive you to town for more.

BRICK. Lacey will get me ——

MARGARET. Lacey's been told not to!

BRICK. I could drive ——

MARGARET. And you lost your driver's license! I'd phone ahead and have you stopped on the highway before you got half way to Ruby Lightfoot's gin mill. I told a lie to Big Daddy, but we can make that lie come true. And then I'll bring you liquor, and we'll get drunk together, here, tonight, in this place that death has come into! What do you say? What do you say, baby?

BRICK. (*Crosses to* l. *side of bed.*) I admire you, Maggie. (*Brick sits on edge of bed. He looks up at the overhead light, then at Margaret. She reaches for the light, turns it out, then she kneels quickly beside Brick at foot of bed.*)

MARGARET. Oh, you weak, beautiful people who give up with such grace. What you need is someone to take hold of you— gently, with love, and hand your life back to you, like something gold you let go of—and I can! I'm determined to do it—and nothing's more determined than a cat on a tin roof—is there? Is there, baby? (*She touches his cheek, gently.*)

CURTAIN

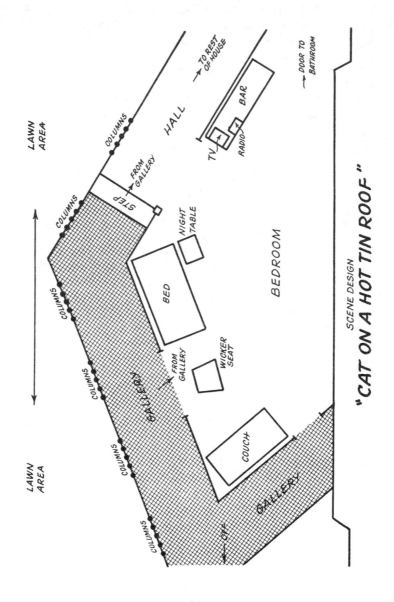

"CAT ON A HOT TIN ROOF"

SCENE DESIGN

PROPERTY LIST

On Stage At Rise, Act I

Bar—TV-radio unit—u. l. Ice bucket, filled with cubes. 3 bottles of "Echo Springs" whiskey, filled, 1 bottle of "Echo Springs" whiskey, half-filled, pitcher of water, wet balled-up bar rag, 2 weighted metal cups (highball glass size), 1 unweighted metal cup (highball glass size), 4 small juice glasses, measuring jigger, double-ended, bar spoon, ashtray, drink ready in glass. 1st shelf—3 unweighted metal cups, highball glass size. 2nd shelf—3 unweighted metal cups, 1 brandy snifter. 3rd shelf (bottom)—cigar box

Shutter door—attached to 1st l. portal—*Act J only*. Silk suit, on hanger, hung on clothes hook behind shutter. Silk shirt, hung over suit, on clothes hook—for Margaret. Bath towel—tacked over top of shutter door

Night table—r. of hall door. Kleenex in box, ash tray, fountain pen, large comb, cuff links—resting on box in table drawer

Double bed—r. of night table, in top corner of set. Blue lace spread with beige underspread, single pillow, d. l. corner, palm fan—u. c., gift box under, tied with ribbon, prop cashmere robe, birthday card in envelope on r. side of box top

Wicker love seat, r. of foot of bed, d. s. of u. r. gallery door

Sofa, covered with horsehair cushion, in u. r. corner of set. Pillow u. s. end, folded blanket, d. s. end, spare crutch under

Off l.

In bath—for Brick: Crutch, water for 1st entrance preparation, bath towel, pair silk pajamas, bedroom slipper—for left foot, resin box—for Margaret

For Mae: Palm fan, archery bow, briefcase, 3 legal folders with papers and map

For Gooper: Small juice glass with whiskey, cigarettes, matches

For Big Mama: Small pillbox on chain (costume), orchid corsage (costume)

For Big Daddy: 4 cigars, matches

For Dr. Baugh: 1 cigar, pocket watch on fob, wrapped hypodermic needle kit

For Daisy: 2 leather pillows

For Sookey: Large sheet of wrapping paper

83

For Sonny: Loaded cap gun
For Dixie: 2-holster gun belt with cap-loaded gun
For Buster: 2 loaded cap guns
For Trixie: Small newspaper roll, birthday cake, candles, loaded cap gun, tapers, matches
Effects—for Stage Manager: Pitch pipe, bottle crash, clock chimes, phone bell, shutters—sound only, barrel—for crash sound

Off r.

For Lacey: 2 filled wine bottles, Fuller's earth, to dust bottles, raincoat
For Rev. Tooker, Dr. Baugh, Dixie: 2 croquet mallets—1 to Dixie later, 2 croquet balls, grass mat
For Mae: Palm fan
For Big Daddy: Walking stick, cashmere robe, slippers, cigar in pocket of robe
For Sonny: Small drum and sticks
For Brightie: Rubber poncho
For Dixie and Trixie: 2 electric sparklers
For Big Mama: Glass of milk
Effects—for Stage Manager: 2 hawk effects, song bird effect, frog effect, thunder drum and mallets, farm bell, glass crash

Act II

Strike: Bathroom door-shutter (carpenter), bar rag from sofa, silk shirt from bed, d. r. corner of bar of bottles, glasses, etc., to place birthday cake

SOUND CUES

BAND	CUE	PAGE	EFFECTS
1	1	14	Hawk cries
1	2	18	Hawk cries
1	3	23	Hawk cries
1	4	24	Hawk cries
1	5	24	Hawk cries
1	6	25	Hawk cries
1	7	25	Hawk cries
2	8	25	Frog calls
3	9	31	Radio Announcer
4	10	32	Sportscaster
5	11	33	Field bell
6	12	41	Clock chimes 11 o'clock
7	13	46	Clock—one chime
8	14	50	Clock—two chimes
1	15	50	Hawk cries
9	16	55	Clock—three chimes
10	17	57	Fireworks, cheers, whistles
11	18	60	Fireworks
12	19	72	Rumble of thunder
13	20	73	Rumble of thunder with wind
12	21	74	Rumble of thunder
12	22	74	Rumble of thunder
14	23	75	Thunder clap, glass crash, barnyard animals in terror, storm sounds
15	24	75	Dog howl
12	25	75	Rumble of thunder
12	26	75	Rumble of thunder
15	27	75	Dog howl
15	28	75	Dog howl
16	29	80	Clock chimes 12

NEW PLAYS

★ **RABBIT HOLE by David Lindsay-Abaire.** Winner of the 2007 Pulitzer Prize. Becca and Howie Corbett have everything a couple could want until a life-shattering accident turns their world upside down. "An intensely emotional examination of grief, laced with wit." *–Variety.* "A transcendent and deeply affecting new play." *–Entertainment Weekly.* "Painstakingly beautiful." *–BackStage.* [2M, 3W] ISBN: 978-0-8222-2154-8

★ **DOUBT, A Parable by John Patrick Shanley.** Winner of the 2005 Pulitzer Prize and Tony Award. Sister Aloysius, a Bronx school principal, takes matters into her own hands when she suspects the young Father Flynn of improper relations with one of the male students. "All the elements come invigoratingly together like clockwork." *–Variety.* "Passionate, exquisite, important, engrossing." *–NY Newsday.* [1M, 3W] ISBN: 978-0-8222-2219-4

★ **THE PILLOWMAN by Martin McDonagh.** In an unnamed totalitarian state, an author of horrific children's stories discovers that someone has been making his stories come true. "A blindingly bright black comedy." *–NY Times.* "McDonagh's least forgiving, bravest play." *–Variety.* "Thoroughly startling and genuinely intimidating." *–Chicago Tribune.* [4M, 5 bit parts (2M, 1W, 1 boy, 1 girl)] ISBN: 978-0-8222-2100-5

★ **GREY GARDENS book by Doug Wright, music by Scott Frankel, lyrics by Michael Korie.** The hilarious and heartbreaking story of Big Edie and Little Edie Bouvier Beale, the eccentric aunt and cousin of Jacqueline Kennedy Onassis, once bright names on the social register who became East Hampton's most notorious recluses. "An experience no passionate theatergoer should miss." *–NY Times.* "A unique and unmissable musical." *–Rolling Stone.* [4M, 3W, 2 girls] ISBN: 978-0-8222-2181-4

★ **THE LITTLE DOG LAUGHED by Douglas Carter Beane.** Mitchell Green could make it big as the hot new leading man in Hollywood if Diane, his agent, could just keep him in the closet. "Devastatingly funny." *–NY Times.* "An out-and-out delight." *–NY Daily News.* "Full of wit and wisdom." *–NY Post.* [2M, 2W] ISBN: 978-0-8222-2226-2

★ **SHINING CITY by Conor McPherson.** A guilt-ridden man reaches out to a therapist after seeing the ghost of his recently deceased wife. "Haunting, inspired and glorious." *–NY Times.* "Simply breathtaking and astonishing." *–Time Out.* "A thoughtful, artful, absorbing new drama." *–Star-Ledger.* [3M, 1W] ISBN: 978-0-8222-2187-6

DRAMATISTS PLAY SERVICE, INC.
440 Park Avenue South, New York, NY 10016   212-683-8960   Fax 212-213-1539
postmaster@dramatists.com   www.dramatists.com